BREATHING UNDER WATER

RICHARD ROHR

BREATHING UNDER WATER

Spirituality
and the
Twelve Steps

Originally published in the United States of America in 2011
by Franciscan Media, Cincinnati, Ohio

First published in Great Britain in 2016

Society for Promoting Christian Knowledge
36 Causton Street
London SW1P 4ST
www.spck.org.uk

Copyright © Richard Rohr 2011, 2016

All rights reserved. No part of this book may be reproduced or transmitted in any form
or by any means, electronic or mechanical, including photocopying, recording, or
by any information storage and retrieval system, without permission in
writing from the publisher.

SPCK does not necessarily endorse the individual views contained in its publications.

The author and publisher have made every effort to ensure that the external website
and email addresses included in this book are correct and up to date at the time
of going to press. The author and publisher are not responsible for the
content, quality or continuing accessibility of the sites.

Scripture quotations are the author's own paraphrase, or his choice from
several translations, particularly *The Jerusalem Bible*, published and copyright ©
1966, 1967 and 1968 by Darton, Longman & Todd Ltd and Doubleday,
a division of Random House, Inc., and used by permission.

British Library Cataloguing-in-Publication Data
A catalogue record for this book is available from the British Library

ISBN 978–0–281–07512–6
eBook ISBN 978–0–281–07513–3

Typeset by Graphicraft Limited, Hong Kong
First printed in Great Britain by Ashford Colour Press
Subsequently digitally printed in Great Britain

eBook by Graphicraft Limited, Hong Kong

Produced on paper from sustainable forests

—————————— DEDICATION ——————————

This book is written for you.

•

——————— CONTENTS ———————

•

•

"I did not come for the healthy, but for those who need a doctor."

—Jesus (Luke 5:31–32)

"You see, Alcohol in Latin is 'spiritus' and you use the same word for the highest religious experience as well as for the most depraving poison."

—Carl Jung's letter to Bill Wilson in 1961,
shortly before Jung's death

•

•

———————— INTRODUCTION ————————

•

"These are the only genuine ideas, the ideas of the ship-wrecked. All the rest is rhetoric, posturing, farce."[1]

— Jose Ortega y Gasset

Almost twenty-five years ago, I gave a set of talks in Cincinnati to link the wisdom of the Twelve Step Program with what St. Francis called "the marrow of the Gospel."[2] I was amazed how obvious and easy a task it was, and was surprised this was not equally obvious to everybody involved in either of these fields. So the least I can hope to do here is to make what seems obvious a bit more obvious.

"Twelve Steppers" sometimes thought they had left the church for the Wednesday night meetings in the basement; and many upstairs in the sanctuary presumed that their "higher" concerns were something different from "those people with problems" down below. The similar messages between the two teachings assure me that we are dealing with a common inspiration from the Holy Spirit and from the same collective unconscious. In fact, I am still convinced that on the practical (read "transformational") level, the Gospel message of Jesus and the Twelve Step message of Bill Wilson are largely the same message, even in some detail, as I will try to show in this book. (I will frequently quote Bill W as the assigned author of the Twelve Steps and the so-called *Big Book* of Alcoholics Anonymous, but I am aware there is some doubt as to who exactly wrote what.)

My original lectures were called "Breathing Under Water," a title taken from a telling poem by Carol Bieleck, R.S.C.J., which seemed to sum up so much of the common message. I quote it here in full:

"Breathing Under Water"

I built my house by the sea.
Not on the sands, mind you;
not on the shifting sand.
And I built it of rock.
A strong house
by a strong sea.
And we got well acquainted, the sea and I.
Good neighbors.
Not that we spoke much.
We met in silences.
Respectful, keeping our distance,
but looking our thoughts across the fence of sand.
Always, the fence of sand our barrier,
always, the sand between.

And then one day,
—and I still don't know how it happened—
the sea came.
Without warning.

Without welcome, even

Not sudden and swift, but a shifting across the sand
  like wine,
less like the flow of water than the flow of blood.
Slow, but coming.
Slow, but flowing like an open wound.
And I thought of flight and I thought of drowning
  and I thought of death.
And while I thought the sea crept higher, till it
  reached my door.
And I knew then, there was neither flight, nor death,
  nor drowning.
That when the sea comes calling you stop being
  neighbors
Well acquainted, friendly-at-a-distance, neighbors
And you give your house for a coral castle,
And you learn to breathe underwater.[3]

The original cassette recordings continued to move over the years, eventually became CDs, and morphed into a second set of talks called "How Do We Breathe Under Water?" done over fifteen years later. People continued to encourage me to put some of these ideas into written form. So, with some added growth and experience, here is my attempt. I hope it can offer all of us *some underwater breathing lessons*—for a culture, and a church, that often appears to be drowning without knowing it. But do not despair. What Ortega y Gasset calls the state of mind of the "shipwrecked" is perhaps a necessary beginning point for any salvation from such drowning.

Connecting the Gospel and the Twelve Steps

Although in this book I will first look at the trapped individual, I will also try to point out the very similar parallels in institutions, cultures, and nations. As organizational consultant and psychotherapist Anne Wilson Schaef said many years ago, our society itself shows all the signs of classic addiction. I began to wonder whether addiction could be one very helpful metaphor for what the biblical tradition called "sin."

I personally am convinced that is the case, which might be the first foundational connection between the Gospel and the Twelve Step Program. How helpful it is to see sin, like addiction, as a *disease*, a very destructive disease, instead of merely something that was culpable, punishable, or "made God unhappy." If sin indeed made God unhappy, it was because *God desires nothing more than our happiness, and wills the healing of our disease.* The healing ministry of Jesus should have made that crystal clear; healing was about all that he did, with much of his teaching illustrating the healings—and vice versa. It is rather amazing that this did not remain at the top of all church agendas.

As Carol Bieleck says in her poem, we cannot stop the drowning waters of our addictive culture from rising, but we must at least see our reality for what it is, seek to properly detach from it, and build a coral castle and learn to breathe under water. The New Testament called it salvation or enlightenment, the Twelve Step Program called it recovery. The trouble is that most Christians pushed this great liberation off into the next world, and many Twelve Steppers settled for

mere sobriety from a substance instead of a real transformation of the self. We have all been the losers, as a result—
waiting around for "enlightenment at gunpoint" (death)
instead of enjoying God's banquet much earlier in life.

The Twelve Step Program parallels, mirrors, and makes
practical the same messages that Jesus gave us, but now
without as much danger of spiritualizing the message and
pushing its effects into a future and metaphysical world. By
the fourth century Christianity had become the official religion of the Roman Empire, which left us needing to *agree* on
its transcendent truth claims (for example, Jesus is God, God
is Trinity, Mary was a virgin, etc.), instead of experiencing the
very practical "steps" of human enlightenment, the central
message of our own transformation into "the divine nature"
(2 Peter 1:4), and bringing about a "new creation" on this
earth (Galatians 6:15). It became theory over practice.

We henceforth concentrated on how to worship Jesus as one
united empire instead of following Jesus in any practical ways
(even though he never once said "worship me" but often said
"follow me"). The emperors, not popes or bishops, convened
the next few councils of the church, and their concerns were
usually not the healing of the masses but a united empire; and
surely not Jesus' clear teaching on nonviolence, simplicity of
lifestyle, and healing those on the edge, which would have
derailed the urgent concerns of an empire, as we see to this day.

Our Christian preoccupation with *metaphysics and the future*
became the avoiding of *the "physics" itself and the present.*

Endless theorizing, and the taking of sides, opinions about which we could be right or wrong, trumped and toppled the universally available gift of the Divine Indwelling, the real "incarnation" which still has the power to change the world.

As Tertullian, sometimes called the first Western theologian (AD 166–225), said, "*Caro salutis cardo,*"[4] *the flesh* is the hinge on which salvation swings and the axis on which it hangs. When Christianity loses its material/physical/earthly interests, it has very little to say about how God actually loves the world into wholeness. In endless arguing about Spirit, we too often avoided both body and soul. Now we suffer the consequences of a bodily addicted and too often soulless society, while still arguing the abstractions of theology and liturgy, and paying out an always available Holy Spirit to the very few who meet all the requirements.

Going Toward the Pain

There is no side to take in the Twelve Step Program! It is not a worthiness contest. *There is only an absolutely necessary starting point! The experience of "powerlessness" is where we all must begin.* And Alcoholics Anonymous (A.A.) is honest and humble enough to state this, just as Jesus himself always went *where the pain was.* Wherever there was human suffering, Jesus was concerned about it *now, and about its healing now.* It is rather amazing and very sad that we pushed it all off into a future reward system for those who were "worthy." As if any of us are.

Is it this human pain that we are afraid of? Powerlessness, the state of the shipwrecked, is an experience we all share anyway, if we are sincere, but Bill Wilson found we are not very good at that either. He called it "denial." It seems we are not that free to be honest, or even aware, because most of our garbage is buried in the unconscious. So it is absolutely essential that we find a spirituality that reaches to that hidden level. If not, nothing really changes.

It is not necessarily bad will or even conscious denial on our part. We just can't see what we are not forced to see. As Jesus put it, we "see the splinter in our brother's or sister's eye and miss the log in our own" (Matthew 7:4–5). The whole deceptive game is revealed in that one brilliant line from Jesus. But we seem to need something to force us to deal with that log. For many, if not most, people the only thing strong enough to force them is some experience of addiction, some moral failure, or some falling over which they are powerless.[5]

We are all spiritually powerless, however, and not just those physically addicted to a substance, which is why I address this book to everyone. Alcoholics just have their powerlessness visible for all to see. The rest of us disguise it in different ways, and overcompensate for our more hidden and subtle addictions and attachments, especially our addiction to our way of *thinking*.

We all take our own pattern of thinking as normative, logical, and surely true, even when it does not fully compute. We keep doing the same thing over and over again, even if it is not working for us. That is the self-destructive, even "demonic," nature of all addiction and of the mind, in particular. *We think we are our thinking, and we even take that thinking as utterly "true," which removes us at least two steps from reality itself.* We really are our own worst enemies, and salvation is primarily from ourselves. It seems humans would sooner die than change or admit that they are mistaken.

This thinking mind, with a certain tit-for-tat rationality, made the Gospel itself into an achievement contest in which "the one with the most willpower wins," even though almost everybody actually loses by the normal criteria. That is how far *the ego* (read "false self" or Paul's word "the flesh") will go to promote and protect itself. It would sooner die than change or admit that it is mistaken. It would sooner live in a win/lose world in which most lose than allow God any win-win victory. Grace is always a humiliation for the ego, it seems.

At that level, organized religion is no longer good news for most people, but bad news indeed. It set us up for the massive atheism, agnosticism, hedonism, and secularism we now see in almost all formerly Christian countries (and in those who just keep up the externals). I now have more people tell me they are "recovering Catholics" than those in recovery from addiction. I am told that for every person that is joining the church, three are leaving. Are these all bad or insincere people? I don't think so. Perhaps we failed to give them the good news they desired, needed, and expected?

"The Vital Spiritual Experience"

On the other hand, the Twelve Step Program often became a program for mere sobriety from a substance, and never moved many toward the "vital spiritual experience" that Bill W deemed absolutely foundational for full recovery.[6] If we can speak of the traditional Christian stages of the spiritual journey as (1) purgation, (2) illumination, and (3) union, too many addicts never seem to get to the second or third stages—any real spiritual illumination of the self—and even fewer get to the rich life of *experienced* union with God. In that, they mirror many mainline Christians, I am sad to say.

The Twelve Step Program has too often stayed at the problem-solving level, and missed out on the ecstasy itself—trustful intimacy with God, or what Jesus consistently called "the wedding banquet." The world was left with the difficult task of trying to live with even more difficult "dry drunks." These are people who do not drink or take drugs anymore, but they drive the rest of us to want to drink by their "all or nothing" thinking, which distorts and destroys most calm and clear communication.

If you think I am being unfair, hear Bill Wilson's comment himself in his later years:

> When A.A. was quite young, a number of eminent psychologists and doctors made an exhaustive study of a good-sized group of so-called problem drinkers. They finally came up with a conclusion that shocked the A.A. members of that time. *These distinguished men had the nerve to say that most of the alcoholics under investigation were still childish, emotionally sensitive, and grandiose.*

How we alcoholics did resent that verdict! We would not believe that our adult dreams were often truly childish. And considering the rough deal life had given us, we felt it perfectly natural that we were sensitive. As to our grandiose behavior, we insisted that we had been possessed of nothing but a high and legitimate ambition to win the battle of life![7]

It is my experience after over forty years as a priest that we could say the same about many well-intentioned Christians and clergy. Their religion has never touched them or healed them at the unconscious level where all of the real motivation, hurts, unforgiveness, anger, wounds, and illusions are stored, hiding—and often fully operative. They never went to "the inner room" where Jesus invited us, and where things hid "secretly" (Matthew 6:6).

Christians are usually sincere and well-intentioned people until you get to any real issues of ego, control, power, money, pleasure, and security. Then they tend to be pretty much like everybody else. We often gave them a bogus version of the Gospel, some fast-food religion, without any deep transformation of the self; and the result has been the spiritual disaster of "Christian" countries that tend to be as consumer-oriented, proud, warlike, racist, class conscious, and addictive as everybody else—and often more so, I am afraid.

People were Catholic, for example, because they were Italian, Spanish, or Irish, not because they "did the steps" or had any "vital spiritual experience" that changed their lives. We must be honest here, and not defensive; the issues are now too grave and too urgent. Our inability to see our personal failures is paralleled by our inability to see our institutional and national sins too. It is the identical and same pattern of addiction and denial. Thank God that Pope John Paul II introduced into our vocabulary words like "structural sin" and "institutional evil." It was not even part of the conversation in most of Christian history up to now, as we exclusively concentrated on "personal" sins. The three sources of evil were traditionally called "the world, the flesh, and the devil." We so concentrated on the flesh that we let the world and "the devil" get off scot-free.[8]

We have our work cut out for us, and the Twelve Step Program made it very clear that it is indeed work, and not fast food or cheap grace. Gospel people need to do their honest inner work, "Steppers" need to "do the steps"; and they both need to know that they are then eating from the very rich and nutritious "marrow of the Gospel."

Four Assumptions About Addiction

I am writing this book, therefore, with these four assumptions:

We are all addicts. Human beings are addictive by nature. Addiction is a modern name and honest description for what the biblical tradition called "sin," and medieval Christians called "passions" or "attachments." They both recognized that serious measures, or practices, were needed to break us out of these illusions and entrapments; in fact the New Testament calls them in some cases "exorcisms"! They knew they were dealing with non-rational evil or "demons."

"Stinking thinking" is the universal addiction. Substance addictions like alcohol and drugs are merely the most visible form of addiction, but actually we are all addicted to our own habitual way of doing anything, our own defenses, and most especially, our patterned way of thinking, or how we process our reality. The very fact we have to say this shows how much we are blinded inside of it. By definition, you can never see or handle what you are addicted to. It is always "hidden" and disguised as something else. As Jesus did with the demon at Gerasa, someone must say, "What is your name?" (Luke 8:30). The problem must be correctly named before the demon can be exorcised. You cannot heal what you do not first acknowledge.

All societies are addicted to themselves and create deep codependency on them. There are shared and agreed-upon addictions in every culture and every institution. These are often the hardest to heal because they do not look like addictions because we have all agreed to be compulsive about the same things and blind to the same problems. The Gospel exposes those lies in every culture: The American addiction to oil, war, and empire; the church's addiction to its own absolute exceptionalism; the poor person's addiction to powerlessness and victimhood; the white person's addiction to superiority; the wealthy person's addiction to entitlement.

Some form of alternative consciousness is the only freedom from this self and from cultural lies. If the universal addiction is to our own pattern of thinking, which is invariably dualistic, the primary spiritual path must be some form of contemplative practice, once just called "prayer," to break down this unhelpful binary system of either-or thinking, and superiority thinking. "Praying" is changing your operating system! This was well recognized in Step 11 of the Twelve Steps.

When religion does not move people to the mystical or nondual level of consciousness[9] it is more a part of the problem than any solution whatsoever. It solidifies angers, creates enemies, and is almost always exclusionary of the most recent definition of "sinner." At this level, it is largely incapable of its supreme task of healing, reconciling, forgiving, and peacemaking. When religion does not give people an inner life or a real prayer life, it is missing its primary vocation.

Let me sum up, then, the foundational ways that I believe Jesus and the Twelve Steps of A.A. are saying the same thing but with different vocabulary:

> We suffer to get well.
> We surrender to win.
> We die to live.
> We give it away to keep it.

This counterintuitive wisdom will forever be resisted as true, denied, and avoided, until it is forced upon us—by some reality over which we are powerless—and if we are honest, we are *all powerless* in the presence of full Reality.

•

CHAPTER ONE

Powerlessness

•

We admitted we were powerless over alcohol—that our lives had become unmanageable.

—Step 1 of the Twelve Steps

•

"Like a weaver, you roll up my life, and cut it from the loom. From dawn to night you are watching my failure. I cry aloud until the morning, but like a lion you crush all my bones. I twitter like a swallow, I moan like a dove."

—Isaiah 38:12–14

"I cannot understand my own behavior. I fail to carry out the very things I want to do, and find myself doing the very things I hate…for although the will to do what is good is in me, the performance is not."

—Romans 7:15,18

"And when Jesus looked at the crowds, he felt sorry for them, because they were harassed and dejected, like sheep without a shepherd."

—Matthew 9:36

•

I must be up front with you. I do not really understand why God created the world this way. I do not know why "power is at its best in weakness" as Paul says, or "it is when I am weak that I am strong" (2 Corinthians 12:9–10). It sure seems like God is some kind of trickster. Perhaps the Divine is playing games with us. God seems to have hidden holiness and wholeness in a secret place where only the humble will find it. Some topsy-turvy God has decided that those on the bottom will be revealed as the true top, and those who try for the top will find nothing of substance there. Why such a disguise? Why such a game of hide-and-seek?

God's Greatest Surprise and Constant Disguise
All I know is that it matches my own observation. I cannot pretend to understand God, but this is what I see: People who have moved from seeming success to seeming success seldom understand success at all, except a very limited version of their own. People who fail to do it right, by even their own definition of right, are those who often break through to enlightenment and compassion. It is still a mystery to me, and

will still be a mystery for you, even if you read this book to the end. The big difference, and it is big, is that you will hopefully be able to accept and even revel in this cosmic economy of grace. It is God's greatest surprise and God's constant disguise, but you only know it to be true by going through it and coming out the other side yourself. You cannot know it by just going to church, reading Scriptures, or listening to someone else talk about it, even if you agree with them.

Until you bottom out, and come to the limits of your own fuel supply, there is no reason for you to switch to a higher octane of fuel. For that is what is happening! Why would you? You will not learn to actively draw upon a Larger Source until your usual resources are depleted and revealed as wanting. In fact, you will not even know there is a Larger Source until your own sources and resources fail you.

Until and unless there is a person, situation, event, idea, conflict, or relationship that you cannot "manage," you will never find the True Manager. So *God makes sure that several things will come your way that you cannot manage on your own.* Self-made people, and all heroic spiritualities, will try to manufacture an even stronger self by willpower and determination—to put them back in charge and seeming control. Usually most people admire this, not realizing the unbending, sometimes proud, and eventually rigid personality that will be the long-term result. They will then need to continue in this pattern of self-created successes and defenses. This pushy response does not normally create loving people, but just people in control and in ever deeper need of control. Eventually, the game is unsustainable, unless you make others, even your whole family, pay the price for your own aggression and self-assertion —which is the common pattern.

More commonly, many Christians whittle down the great Gospel to some moral issue over which they can feel totally triumphant and superior, and which usually asks nothing of them personally. The ego always insists on moral high ground, or as Paul brilliantly puts it, "sin takes advantage of commandments to mislead me, and through obeying commandments kills me" (Romans 7:11,13). This is a really quite extraordinary piece of insight on Paul's part, one which I would not believe myself were the disguise not so common (e.g., celibate priests focusing on birth control and abortion as the core of evil, heterosexuals seeing gay marriage as the ultimate threat to society, liberals invested in some current political correctness while living lives of rather total isolation from the actual suffering of the world, Bible thumpers ignoring most of the Bible when it asks *them* to change, a nation of immigrants being anti-immigrant, etc.). We see that the ego is still in charge, and it just wears different disguises on both the Left and on the Right side of most groups and most issues.

It is the imperial ego that has to go, and only powerlessness can do the job correctly. Bill W recognized that very early in his Twelve Step Program. Otherwise, we try to engineer our own transformation by our own rules and by our own power, which is by definition, therefore, not transformation! It seems we can in no way engineer or steer our own conversion. If we try to change our ego with the help of our ego, we only have a better-disguised ego! As physicist Albert Einstein frequently said in a different way: No problem can be solved by the same consciousness that caused the problem in the first place.

Jesus used the metaphors of a "grain of wheat" or a "branch cut off from the vine" for this arrogant ego; Paul used the unfortunate word "flesh," which made most think he was talking about the body. So some Bible translations now call it "self-indulgence," which is much closer to the meaning. But both Jesus and Paul were pointing to the isolated and protected small self. And they both said it has to go: "Unless the grain of wheat falls on the ground and dies, it remains only a single grain; but if it dies, it will yield a rich harvest" (John 12:24). For Paul, the "flesh" or ego cannot get you where you want to go (Galatians 5:19). Its concerns are too small and too selfish.

An ego response is *always* an inadequate or even wrong response to the moment. It will not deepen or broaden life, love, or inner laughter. Your ego self is *always* attached to mere externals, since it has no inner substance itself. The ego defines itself by its attachments and revulsions. The soul does not attach nor does it hate; *it desires and loves and lets go.* Please think about that, it can change your very notion of religion.

All Mature Spirituality Is About Letting Go

As many teachers of the Twelve Steps have said, the first Step is probably the hardest, the most denied, and the most avoided. So the whole process never takes off! No one likes to die to who they think they are. Their "false self" is all they have, as Trappist monk and spiritual writer Thomas Merton writes in *New Seeds of Contemplation*. (This classic of Merton's is still probably the best clarification of what we mean by the true self and the false self.) Letting go is not in anybody's program for happiness, and yet *all mature spirituality, in one sense or another, is about letting go and unlearning.* You can take that as an absolute. As German mystic-philosopher Meister Eckhart said, the spiritual life has much more to do with subtraction than it does with addition.

What the ego hates more than anything else in the world is to change—even when the present situation is not working or is horrible. Instead, *we do more and more of what does not work,* as many others have rightly said about addicts, and, I would say, about all of us. The reason we do anything one more time is because the last time did not really satisfy us deeply. As English poet W.H. Auden put it in "Apropos of Many Things": "We would rather be ruined than changed. We would rather die in our dread than climb the cross of the present and let our illusions die."

•

CHAPTER TWO

Desperate Desiring

•

Came to believe that a Power greater than ourselves could restore us to sanity.

—*Step 2 of the Twelve Steps*

•

"The God of old is still your refuge. This God has everlasting arms that can drive out the enemy before you."

—*Deuteronomy 33:27*

"Yes, we are carrying our own death warrant with us, but it is teaching us not to rely on ourselves, but on a God whose task is to raise the dead to life."

—*2 Corinthians 1:9*

"While he was still a long way off, the father saw him and was moved with pity. He ran to the boy, clasped him in his arms and kissed him tenderly."

—*Luke 15:21*

•

Step 2 is the necessary longing, delaying, and backsliding that invariably precedes the full-blown leap of faith. The statement is wise enough to use an active verb to describe this step: "We *came to believe* that a Power greater than ourselves could restore us to sanity." The surrender of faith does not happen in one moment but is an extended journey, a trust walk, a gradual letting go, unlearning, and handing over. No one does it on the first or even second try. Desire and longing must be significantly deepened and broadened.

To finally surrender ourselves to healing, we have to have three spaces opened up within us—and all at the same time: our opinionated head, our closed-down heart, and our defensive and defended body. That is the work of spirituality—and it is work. Yes, it is finally the work of "a Power greater than ourselves," and it will lead to great *luminosity* and depth of seeing. That is why true faith is one of the most holistic and free actions a human can perform. It leads to such broad and deep perception, that most traditions would just call it "light."

Remember, Jesus said that *we* were the light of the world also (Matthew 5:14) and not just himself (John 8:12). Christians often forget this. Such luminous seeing is quite the opposite of the closed-minded, dead heart, body-denying thing that much religion has allowed faith to become. As you have surely heard before, "Religion is lived by people who are afraid of hell. Spirituality is lived by people who have been through hell."

The innocuous mental belief systems of much religion are probably the major cause of atheism in the world today, because people see that they have not generally created people who are more strong, caring, or creative than other groups—and often a lot worse. I wish I did not have to say that, but religion either produces the very best people or the very worst. Jesus makes this point in many settings and stories. Mere mental belief systems split people apart, whereas actual faith puts all our parts (body, heart, head) on notice and on call, and offers us a new broadband station, with full surround sound, instead of a static-filled monotone. Honestly, it takes major surgery and much of one's life to get head, heart, and body to put down their defenses, their false programs for happiness, and their many forms of resistance to what is right in front of them. This is the meat and the muscle of the whole conversion process.

As hard as it is to believe, many formally religious people do not believe in the reality of Spirit in any active or effective way. They think it is their job to somehow teach, introduce, or "win" Spirit, and they never get around to enjoying what is already and always there—and actively on their side. Walter Wink, a professor of biblical interpretation, calls it the mere "theological" worldview as opposed to the incarnational worldview, which is authentic Christianity.[1] *When all of you is there, you will know. When all of you is present, the banquet will begin.*

But as Jesus said in his many banquet stories, we all find our very proper excuses why *not* to come to anything so free, so spacious, and so available to all. "There is still more room!" he says at the end. (See Luke 14:15–24.) Many seem to be put off by the fact that the invitation list includes "both good and bad alike" (Matthew 22:10). The ego, or the "flesh," would prefer to join a private country club or a gated community, whereas Peter will say, "God has made it clear to me that I must not call anyone profane or unclean" (Acts 10:28), although it took him a while to get there himself.

When all three inner spaces are open and listening together, we can always be present. *To be present is to know what you need to know in the moment.* To be present to something is to allow the moment, the person, the idea, or the situation to change *you.*

Opening Three Inner Spaces

I will describe the three openings briefly here, but I am encouraging any reader to seek other resources to deepen each of these disciplines.

To keep the mind space open, we need some form of contemplative or meditation practice. This has been the most neglected in recent centuries, substituting the mere reciting and "saying" of prayers, which is not the same as a contemplative mind, and often merely confirms us in our superior or fear-based system. Step 11 was wise enough to name "prayer and meditation" as necessary to the process. I personally describe contemplation as "non-dual consciousness" and find that it is necessary to overcome the "stinking thinking" of most addicts, which tends to be "all or nothing thinking."[2] One could say that authentic spirituality is invariably a matter of *emptying the mind and filling the heart* at the same time.

To keep the heart space open, we need several things. First, we almost all need some healing in regard to our carried hurts from the past. The church's somewhat strange word for this was "original sin," which we were told was not something we were personally guilty of but was something that was *done to us* and passed from generation to generation. No point in blaming anybody. If it was not one thing, it was another. The Enneagram is one marvelous spiritual tool that names the nine most common "programs for happiness" or strategies for survival. It reveals that we are all wounded in our "feeling function" in one way or another. Each type is invariably half right but also half wrong, and it is important that we recognize the half-wrong side, so the good side can be set free.[3] Also, we need to be in right relationship with people, so that other people can love us and touch us at deeper levels, and so we can love and touch them. Nothing else opens up the heart space in such a positive and ongoing way. Fortunately, Steps 4 through 10 are precisely named to make that possible, and we will talk about this more in subsequent chapters.

Finally, I think the heart space is often opened by "right brain" activities[4] such as music, art, dance, nature, fasting, poetry, games, life-affirming sexuality, and, of course, the art of relationship itself. Mass murderers are invariably loners who participate in none of these things but merely ruminate and retreat to their head and their explanations.

I can think of times when I was celebrating Mass in proper form but with a hidden cold heart, and only when I moved into the congregation and received their genuine smiles and warm hugs did I even realize that my heart had been hardened before. Suddenly it was caring and connecting again. That is the rub of any conversion experience: You only know how much you needed it when you are on the other side! That is why you need the tenacity of faith and hope to carry you across to most transformational experiences. When you can let others actually influence you and change you, your heart space is open.

And to be fully honest, I think your heart needs to be broken, and broken open, at least once to have a heart at all or to have a heart for others. As Simeon told Mary, "A sword will pierce your heart, so that the secret thoughts of many will be laid bare" (Luke 2:35).

To keep our bodies less defended, to live in our body right now, to be present to others in a cellular way, is also the work of healing of past hurts and the many memories that seem to store themselves in the body. The body seems to never stop offering its messages; but fortunately, the body never lies, even though the mind will deceive you constantly. Zen practitioners tend to be well-trained in seeing this. It is very telling that Jesus usually physically touched people when he healed them; he knew where the memory and hurt was lodged, and it was in the body itself.

Any massage therapist knows the power of healing touch, and surely it is part of the function of healthy sexual encounters, exercise, the importance of hugging, and why it is so important to protect children from any negative or fearful body messages. The body knows and the body remembers.

It has always deeply disappointed me that the Christian religion was the only one that believed God became a human body, and yet we have had such deficient and frankly negative attitudes toward embodiment, the physical world, sexuality, emotions, animals, healthy physical practices like yoga, and nature itself. It often seems to me that Western Christianity has been much more formed by Plato (body and soul are at war) than by Jesus (body and soul are already one). For many of us the body is more *repressed and denied* than even the mind or the heart.

The body is like the ignored middle child in a family unit, and so now it is having its revenge through so much compulsive eating, sexuality, anorexia, and addiction, plus a wholesale disregard for the physical planet, animals, water, and healthy foods.[5] In every way, we seem to be fouling our own nest, because after all, this nest does not really matter, salvation is merely "an evacuation plan for the next world." There has been little belief in what the Bible offers, which is both a new heaven and a new earth too (Revelation 21:1).

So the work of spirituality is the ongoing liberation of head, heart, and body, toward full luminous seeing and living, and not a mere mental "decision for Jesus" or the one-time insurance policy of sacraments received. Most head churches do not touch the heart, most heart churches do not bother with the head, and almost all of them ignore the body as if of no account. Further, the head churches are usually not contemplative, the heart churches have little discrimination or training in the more subtle emotions whereby we see truthfully, and the body people have either left the church or, even worse, stay in the pew but do not take it seriously as anything real, urgent, or wonderful.

Reconnecting Head, Heart, and Body

If we are to come to believe that a Power greater than ourselves can restore us to sanity, then we will come to that belief by developing the capacity for a *simple, clear, and uncluttered presence*. Those who can be present with head, heart, and body at the same time will always encounter *The Presence*, whether they call it God or not. For the most part, those skills are learned by letting life come at us on its own terms, and not resisting the wonderful underlying Mystery that is every-where, all the time, and offered to us too. "God comes to us disguised as our life," as spiritual writer and retreat leader Paula D'Arcy so beautifully puts it in her talks and retreats.

All we can do is keep out of the way, note, and weep over our defensive behaviors, keep our various centers from closing down—and the Presence that is surely the Highest Power is then obvious, all-embracing, and immediately effec-tive. The immediate embrace is from God's side, the ineffec-tiveness is whatever time it takes for us to "come to believe," which is the slow and gradual healing and reconnecting of head, heart, and body so they can operate as *one*. Both move-ments are crucial: the healing of ourselves and the healing of our always limited and even toxic image of God. This, of itself, will often reconnect all three parts of our humanity into a marvelous receiving station. A "true God" experience really does save us, because it is always better than we thought we could expect or earn.[6]

Let's end with a blessing from St. Paul who recognized these three parts of the human person in his very first letter: "May the God of peace make you whole and holy, may you be kept safe in body, heart, and mind, and thus ready for the pres-ence. God has called you and will not fail you" (1 Thessalonians 5:23).

CHAPTER THREE

Sweet Surrender

·

Made a decision to turn our will and our lives over to the care of God *as we understood God.*

> —*Step 3 of the Twelve Steps*

·

"O, come to the water all you who are thirsty. Though you have no money, come! Buy corn without money, and eat; and, at no cost, wine and milk. Why spend money on what is not bread, your wages on what fails to satisfy?"

> —*Isaiah 55:1–2*

"Work for your salvation in fear and trembling. It is God, for his own loving purposes, who puts both the will and the action into you."

> —*Philippians 2:12–13*

"Ask, and it will be given to you; search and you will find; knock, and the door will be opened to you. For the one who asks always receives; the one who searches always finds; the one who knocks will always have the door opened."

> —*Matthew 7:7–8*

·

Some think that the most helpful of the personal stories in A.A.'s *Big Book* is the one entitled "Acceptance was the Answer." I am sure different stories move different people, depending on their temperament and the stage of their own journey when they read it. But surely Step 3 on acceptance and surrender is quite succinct and telling, and cuts to the chase. It gives new meaning to the word "mercy killing." Surrender will always feel like dying, and yet it is the necessary path to liberation. Many excellent books have been written in recent years on "the art of dying." Stephen Levine led the parade in the early 1980s, but now many have expanded the field, and it is almost becoming its own theological source.[1] It tells me we are surely growing up spiritually.

How long it takes each of us to just *accept*—to accept what is, to accept ourselves, others, the past, our own mistakes, and the imperfection and idiosyncrasies of almost everything. It reveals our basic resistance to life, a terrible contraction at our core or, as Henri Nouwen, a Catholic priest and writer, told me personally once, "our endless capacity for self loathing." Acceptance is not our mode nearly as much as aggression, resistance, fight, or flight. None of them achieve the deep and lasting results of true acceptance and peaceful surrender. It becomes the strangest and strongest kind of power. You see, surrender is not "giving up," as we tend to think, nearly as much as it is a "giving to" the moment, the event, the person, and the situation.

As many have said, "What you resist, persists." This became the groundwork of most nonviolent training, and yet it took us until the twentieth century to believe what Jesus had taught two thousand years ago in a most shocking and incomprehensible line: "Offer the wicked man no resistance" (Matthew 5:39). How could that be wise or true? Why did St. Francis, Gandhi, and Martin Luther King, Jr., agree while most of the rest of us missed the point? Dualistic minds tend to miss spiritual points, but we will talk about this more in a later chapter.

Our inner blockage to "turning our will over" is only overcome by a *decision*. It will not usually happen with a feeling, or a mere idea, or a religious Scripture like the ones above. It is the will itself, our stubborn and self-defeating willfulness that must be first converted and handed over. It does not surrender easily and usually only when it is demanded of us by partners, parents, children, health, or circumstances. We see our ingrained "will to power" already in two-year-olds and teenagers, when it is only getting started. By the time we are "adults," we have all taken control and tried to engineer our own lives in every way possible. In fact, our culture does not respect people who do not "take control."

We each have our inner program for happiness, our plans by which we can be secure, esteemed, and in control, and are blissfully unaware that these cannot work for us for the long haul—without our becoming more and more control freaks ourselves. Something has to break our primary addiction, which is to our own power and our false programs for happiness. Here is the incestuous cycle of the ego: "I want to have power" > "I will take control" >"I will always be right" >"See, I am indeed powerful!" This is the vicious circle of the will to power. It does not create happy people, nor happy people around them.

Any foundational handing over of our *will to power* is previous and prior to any belief system whatsoever. In fact, I would say what makes so much religion so innocuous, ineffective, and even unexciting is that there has seldom been a concrete "decision to turn our lives over to the care of God," even in many people who go to church, temple, or mosque. I have been in religious circles all my life and usually find willfulness run rampant in monasteries, convents, chancery offices, and among priests and prelates, ordinary laity, and at church meetings. In fact, there are about the same percentage of people who have actually handed over their will to God in most church circles as there are people I meet at many "secular" gatherings. It is really quite disappointing that we all could be that successful at missing the major point. Islam even means "surrender" and yet finds it hard to surrender to the truth about terrorism, suicide bombers, and its own will to power. Religious surrender, I am afraid, is often to status itself and the *status quo* instead of to the full truth of a situation. So Bill Wilson was wise enough to make it a clear Step 3 in the program.

But Jesus made it step one, you might say: "If anyone wants to follow me, let him *renounce himself* [or herself!]" (Mark 8:34; Luke 9:23; Matthew 16:4). Have we ever really heard that? It is clear in all of the Gospels: "Renouncing the self!" What could Jesus possibly mean or intend by such absolute and irresponsible language? Is this what Buddhists are trying to do in meditation? Of course! I am pretty sure that Jesus meant exactly what Bill W means in Step 3: a radical surrendering of our will to Another whom we trust more than ourselves. Buddhists just stopped arguing about the personal name of to *whom* they were surrendering, but they often do much better about the *how* of actually surrendering their mental ego and their control needs. Christians and Jews sort of avoided that foundational renunciation.

The Myth of Sacrifice

Now do you know what is the most common and, in fact, almost universal, substitute for renouncing our will? Dedicated people have made it into its own form of religion, and I will call it "*the myth of heroic*" *sacrifice.* The common way of renouncing the self, while not really renouncing the self at all,

is being *sacrificial!* It looks so generous and loving, and sometimes it is. But usually it is still all about me. It is the classic
"first half of life" gesture[2] that gives the self boundaries, identity, superiority, definition, admiration, and a real control of
the scene.

Who can argue with a sacrificial person? It has driven most
of the wars, and the romanticization of war, in all of human
history, on both sides. It serves those with power that the
common folks all believe mightily in sacrifice, while far too
often their own sons and daughters never go to war or work
at all. "Personal sacrifice" creates the Olympics and *American
Idol,* many heroic projects, and many wonderful people. It is
just *not* the Gospel, but only its most common substitute.[3]

You see, there is a love that sincerely seeks the spiritual good
of others, and there is a love that is seeking superiority, admiration, and control for itself, even and most especially by
doing "good" and heroic things. Maybe we have to see it in its
full-blown sick state to catch the problem. Suicide bombers
are sacrificial, most resentful people are very sacrificial at one
or another level, the manipulative mother is invariably sacrificial, all codependents are sacrificial, a phenomenon so
common that it created its own group called Al-Anon.

"Codependency" was the disease of those who supported
and contributed to others' disease by what we call "enabling"
behavior. Sometimes the enabler is sicker than the alcoholic
and does not know what to do when the alcoholic enters
recovery. Like all heroic sacrifice, codependent behavior was

so well disguised that it took us until the last century to give it a name—and yet it is everywhere. Codependency studies made us aware that much love is actually not love at all, but its most clever and bogus disguise. So much that is un-love and non-love, and even manipulative "love," cannot be seen or addressed because it is so dang sacrificial. Your hands are well tied.

Codependents end up being just as unhealthy as the addict, while thinking of themselves as strong, generous, and loving. The martyr complex reveals this false side of love and, yes, I think it even applies to some of the martyrs in the church. Some of them, even some of my brother Franciscans, did everything they could to get others to hate and kill them, so they could be sacrificial and be proclaimed martyrs and saints. No wonder Jesus said, "Unless your holiness surpasses that of the scribes and Pharisees, you cannot enter the kingdom of heaven" (Matthew 5:20). In other words, there is an early stage "holiness" that looks like the real thing, but it isn't. This is sacrificial religion, on which the scribes and Pharisees in every group pride themselves.

All zealots and "true believers" tend to be immensely sacrificial on one highly visible level, and fool almost everybody. "I sacrifice myself by obeying these laws and attending these services or even serving the poor" and by being more heroic than you are, they might think. Often they do not love God or others in such heroic "obedience," they are merely seeking moral high ground for themselves and the social esteem that comes with it. (See Luke 18:11–12.) Or as Paul puts it, "I can give my body to be burned, but without love, it is worth nothing" (1 Corinthians 13:3). *Most bogus religion, in my opinion, is highly sacrificial in one or another visible way, but not loving at all.* Yet it fools most people. I will not dare to name names here, but you can fill in the blanks.

It is a common disguise in every religion of the world. The Jewish Pharisees are merely a stand-in for all of us at the lower levels, whereas Jesus is the Jewish stand-in for all of us at the highest level. He affirms full love of God and love of neighbor, and says, "This is far more important than offering any temple holocaust or sacrifice" (Mark 12:33). In several contexts he quotes Hosea the prophet (6:6), saying, "Go, learn the meaning of the words, what I want is mercy, not [your dang!] sacrifices!" (Matthew 9:13, 12:7). He seems to use this quote in several contexts to counter people who are righteous and judgmental, and the holier-than-thou types who are judging him and his disciples for not being "sacrificial" enough.

The Genius of the Twelve Steps

The absolute genius of the Twelve Steps is that it refuses to bless and reward what looks like any moral worthiness game or mere heroic willpower. It spotted the counterfeit and "drags it publicly behind it in a triumphal parade" (Colossians 2:15). With Gospel brilliance and insight, A.A. says that the starting point and, in fact, the continuing point, *is not any kind of worthiness at all but in fact unworthiness!* ("I am an alcoholic!") Suddenly religion loses all capacity for elitism and is democratic to the bone. This is what Jesus affirmed in prostitutes, drunkards, and tax collectors, and what Paul praised when he said, "It is when I am weak that I am strong" (2 Corinthians 12:10). When the churches forget their own Gospel message, the Holy Spirit sneaks in through the ducts and the air vents. A.A. meetings have been very good ductwork, allowing fresh air both in and out of many musty and mildewed churches.

False sacrifice is an actual avoidance of any real "renouncing" of the self, while looking generous or dedicated. This is also revealed in Jesus' insistence that the temple has to go. The temple is the metaphor for sacrificial religion in his time, and explains why he vigorously releases the animals penned up for sacrifice, and all of the "selling and buying" of God (Matthew 21:12) that follows from the sacrificial mind. This is why Jesus mocks the people putting "a great deal" of their money into the temple "treasury" (Mark 12:41) and praises the widow who gives her "mite." As French philosopher and writer René Girard convincingly argued[4] Jesus came to proclaim the death of all sacrificial religion! He ended it "once and for all by offering himself" (Hebrews 7:27), and "abolished the first sort of sacrifice to replace it with a second" (Hebrews 10:9). Once you see this pattern, it is very hard *not* to see it for the rest of your life.

Sacrificial religion was all exposed in Jesus' response to any mechanical or mercenary notion of religion, but we soon went right back to it in many Catholic, Orthodox, and Protestant forms, because the old ego will always prefer an economy of merit and sacrifice to any economy of grace and unearned love, where we have no control. The first one makes us feel heroic and worthy, the second one makes us mere "fools" for Christ as Paul puts it, "those who are nothing at all to show up those who are everything" (1 Corinthians 1:17–31). I know Paul might say a few strange things, but he did understand and teach the marrow of the Gospel. And there it is!

It is no surprise that we could not "turn our will and our lives over to God as we understood him"—because we understood God's love as tit for tat and *quid pro quo!* As long as the spiritual journey was a moral achievement contest, none of us felt worthy, ready, or able to come forward. And many who did come forward did so by splitting themselves, and by denying their own ego and shadow self, and then imposing it on others.

"As We Understand God"

We wasted years of history arguing over whose God was best or true, instead of actually meeting *the always best and true God of love, forgiveness, and mercy.* A.A. was smart enough to avoid this unnecessary obstacle by simply saying "God as we understood Him," trusting that anyone in need of mercy as much as addicts are would surely need and meet a merciful God. If they fail to encounter this Higher healing Power, the whole process grinds to a bitter halt, since we can only show mercy if mercy has been shown to us (Luke 6:36–38). We can only live inside the flow of forgiveness if we have stood under the constant waterfall of needed forgiveness ourselves. *Only hour by hour gratitude is strong enough to overcome all temptations to resentment.*

You will never turn your will and your life over to any other kind of God except a loving and merciful One. Why would you? But now that you know, *why would you not?* At this point it is not sacrifice, or the resentment that often goes with being sacrificial, that motivates you.

Friedrich Nietzsche, the German philosopher, said that what he resented in most Christians was what he perceived as a constant underlying *resentment:* (1) a denied resentment toward God for demanding sacrifice, (2) toward others for not appreciating our sacrifice, (3) sacrificing as much as we sacrifice, (4) and a resentment toward others for not having to do it! There is much evidence of this passive-aggressive stance in many religious people, but not in all, thank God.

We have been graced for a truly sweet surrender, if we can *radically accept being radically accepted—for nothing!* "Or grace would not be grace at all"! (Romans 11:6). As my father, St. Francis, put it, when the heart is pure, "Love responds to Love alone" and has little to do with duty, obligation, requirement, or heroic anything. It is easy to surrender when you know that nothing but Love and Mercy is on the other side.

CHAPTER FOUR

A Good Lamp

•

Made a searching and fearless moral inventory of ourselves.

—*Step 4 of the Twelve Steps*

•

"Sacrifice gives you no pleasure, were I to offer a holocaust, you would not have it. My sacrifice is this broken spirit. You will never scorn a crushed and broken heart."

—*Psalm 50:16–17*

"If inside you have the bitterness of jealousy, or a selfish ambition, never make any false claims for yourself or cover up the truth with lies."

—*James 3:14*

"Be awake and pray that you pass the test. The spirit is willing, but the flesh is weak."

—*Matthew 26:41*

•

Those who were raised in highly moral families, or with a strict religious upbringing, will usually recoil at Step 4. They are so tired of judging themselves—and the judgmentalism toward others that comes with it—that they tend to resist any "searching and fearless moral inventory." Perhaps it did not work for them in the past but only made them more self-preoccupied, and in a negative way besides. "Analysis is paralysis" is surely true for many people.

In fact, I am convinced that some people are driven to addictions to quiet their constant inner critic; it only gives them ever another thing to hate themselves for![1] What a vicious cycle, and honestly not an uncommon one. The internalized voices of a demanding parent, a rigid culture, or a finger-waving church, persist long after the parent is gone, we move to another country, or leave the church. We are now our own problem. That, in fact, is the final value of a moral inventory. Moral scrutiny is not to discover how good or bad I am and regain some moral high ground, but it is to begin some honest "shadow boxing" which is at the heart of all spiritual awakening. Yes, "the truth will set you free" as Jesus says (John 8:32), but first it tends to make you miserable. The medieval spiritual writers called it *compunction*, the necessary sadness and humiliation that comes from seeing one's own failures and weaknesses. Without confidence in a Greater Love, none of us will have the courage to go inside, nor should we. It merely becomes silly scrupulosity (2 Timothy 3:6) and not any mature development of conscience or social awareness.

People only come to deeper consciousness *by intentional struggles with contradictions, conflicts, inconsistencies, inner confusions,* and what the biblical tradition calls "sin" or moral failure. Starting with Adam and Eve, there seems to be a necessary "transgression" that sets the whole human story into motion. In Paul's brilliant exposé on the spiritual function of law, his Letter to the Romans, he actually says that "the law was given to multiply the opportunities of falling!" Now deal with that one. And then he adds "so that grace can even be greater" (5:20–21)! *God actually relishes the vacuum, which God knows God alone can fill.* St. Thérèse of Lisieux called this her "little way," which is nothing other than the Gospel itself. "Whoever is a little one, let him come to me" (Proverbs 9:4) became her mantra and her message.

In other words, the goal is actually not the perfect avoidance of all sin, which is not possible anyway (1 John 1:8–9; Romans 5:12), but *the struggle itself,* and the encounter and wisdom that comes from it. Law and failure create the foil, which creates the conflict, which leads to a very different kind of victory than any of us expected. Not perfect moral victory, not moral superiority, but just *luminosity of awareness and compassion for the world*, which becomes our real moral victory. Alcoholics after thirty years in perfect recovery are still imperfect and still alcoholic, and they know it, which makes all the difference. Paul dares to say that "God has imprisoned all people in their own disobedience so that God can show mercy to all people" (Romans 11:32). It feels like a Divine catch-22, but instead of a no-win situation, it feels more like a "lose-win" situation or even a "win-win." Not a double bind but a double release. No wonder they called it the true "good news!" God has trapped us all inside of certain grace and enclosed all things human in a constant need for mercy.

So shadow boxing, a "searching and fearless moral inventory," is for the sake of truth and humility and generosity of spirit, not vengeance on the self or some kind of total victory over the self. Seeing and naming our actual faults is probably not so much a gift to us—although it is—as it is to those around us. As my Franciscan novice master said to me as a young man, "We must try to make it easier for others to love us." I am sure I needed that advice! People who are more transparent and admitting of their blind spots and personality flaws are actually quite easy to love and be with. None of us need or expect perfect people around us, but we do want people who can be up front and honest about their mistakes and limitations, and hopefully grow from them.

Ongoing Shadow Boxing Is Absolutely Necessary

In that, I think humans are certainly "created in the image and likeness of God" (Genesis 1:26) because that is what God appears to want too: Simple honesty and humility. There is no other way to read Jesus' stories of the prodigal son (Luke 15:11–32) or the publican and the Pharisee (Luke 18:9–14). In each story, the one who did wrong ends up being right— simply because he is honest about it. How have we been able to miss that important point? I suspect it is because the ego wants to think well of itself and deny any shadow material. Only the soul knows that we grow best in the shadowlands. We are blinded inside of either total light or total darkness, but "the light shines on inside the darkness, and it is a light that darkness cannot overcome" (John 1:5). In darkness we find and ever long for more light.

Your shadow self is not your evil self. It is just that part of you that you do not want to see, your unacceptable self by reason of nature, nurture, and choice. That bit of chosen blindness, or what A.A. calls denial, is what allows us to do evil and cruel things—without recognizing them as evil or cruel. So ongoing shadow boxing is absolutely necessary because we all have a well-denied shadow self. We all have that which we cannot see, will not see, dare not see. It would destroy our public and personal self-image.

The more you are attached to any *persona* ("stage mask" in Greek) whatsoever, bad or good, any chosen and preferred self-image, the more shadow self you will have. So we

absolutely need conflicts, relationship difficulties, moral failures, defeats to our grandiosity, even seeming enemies, or we
will have no way to ever spot or track our shadow self. They
are our necessary mirrors. Isn't that sort of a surprise? And
even then, we usually catch it out of the corner of our eye—
in a graced insight and gifted moment of inner freedom.

Let's draw this together with another marvelous quote from
Jesus, who seems to have preceded modern depth psychology
and Step 4 by two thousand years. He says, "Why do you
observe the splinter in your brother's eyes and never notice
the plank in your own? How dare you say to your sister 'Let
me take the splinter out of your eye,' when all the time there
is a log in your own? Take the log out of your own eye first,
and then you will see clearly enough to take the splinter out
of your brother's or sister's eye" (Matthew 7:4–5).

Step 4 is about seeing your own log first, so you can stop
blaming, accusing, and denying, and thus displacing the
problem. It is about *seeing* truthfully and fully. Note that Jesus
does not just praise good moral behavior or criticize immoral
behavior, as you might expect from a lesser teacher, but
instead he talks about *something caught in the eye*. He knows that
if you *see* rightly, the actions and behavior will eventually take
care of themselves. The game is over once we see clearly
because evil succeeds only by disguising itself as good, necessary, or helpful. No one consciously does evil. The very fact
that anyone can do stupid, cruel, or destructive things shows
they are at that moment *unconscious and unaware*. Think about

that: Evil proceeds from a lack of consciousness.

Jesus also says shortly before, "The lamp of the body is the eye. If your eye is sound, your whole body will be filled with light. But if your eye is diseased, your whole body will be darkness. And if the lamp within you is, in fact, darkness, what darkness that will be" (Matthew 6:22–23). Step 4 is about creating a good and trustworthy lamp inside of us that reflects and reveals what is really there, knowing that "anything exposed to the light will itself become light" (Ephesians 5:14). Somehow *goodness is transferred by radiance, reflection, and resonance with another goodness,* more than by any act of self-achievement. We do not pull ourselves up; we are pulled.

God does not directly destroy evil, the way our heroic and dualistic minds would like to imagine. God is much wiser, wastes nothing, and includes everything. The God of the Bible is best known for transmuting and transforming our very evils into *our own more perfect good.* God uses our sins in our own favor! God brings us—through failure—from unconsciousness to ever-deeper consciousness and conscience. How could that not be good news for just about everybody?

———————— CHAPTER FIVE ————————

•

Accountability **IS** *Sustainability*

•

Admitted to God, to ourselves and to another human being the exact nature of our wrongs.

—*Step 5 of the Twelve Steps*

•

"All the time I kept silent and my bones wasted away. I groaned day in and day out, my heart grew parched as stubble in summer drought, and at last I admitted to you that I had sinned and no longer concealed my guilt."

—*Psalm 32:3–5*

"So confess your sins to one another, and pray for one another, and this will cure you."

—*James 5:16*

"If you forgive others their sins, they are indeed forgiven. If you withhold forgiveness from one another, they are held bound."

—*John 20:23*

•

Almost all religion, and all cultures that I know of, have believed in one way or another that sin and evil are to be punished, and retribution is to be demanded of the sinner in this world—and usually the next world too. It is a dualistic system of reward and punishment, good guys and bad guys, and makes perfect sense to the ego. I call it the normal economy of merit or "meritocracy," and it is the best that prisons, courtrooms, wars, lawyers, and even most of the church, which should know better, can do.

The revelation from the cross and the Twelve Steps, however, believes that sin and failure are, in fact, *the setting and opportunity for the transformation and enlightenment of the offender*—and then the future will take care of itself. It is a mystery that makes sense to the soul and is entirely an "economy of grace," which makes sense only to those who have experienced it.

The first is a system of *retributive justice* and has controlled the story line of 99 percent of history. The second is called *restorative justice* and has always been a small minority position, even though it is the clear and revolutionary pattern of Jesus before, during, and after the crucifixion. It seems history could not see what it was not ready to see; but in our time more and more are ready and willing to understand. One cannot help but believe there is an evolution of human and spiritual consciousness. "Spiral Dynamics" is one of the many fine attempts today to describe this evolution of consciousness. Others speak of "The Great Turning," "The Shift," "Integral Theory," or "The Work." All are recognizing that history is moving forward, even if by fits and starts, and even many steps backwards.

As any good therapist will tell you, *you cannot heal what you do not acknowledge,* and what you do not consciously acknowledge will remain in control of you from within, festering and destroying you and those around you. Quote 70 in the *Gospel of Thomas* is many peoples' favorite. It has Jesus saying, "If you bring forth that which is within you, it will save you. If you do not bring it forth, it will destroy you." In Step 5 of the Twelve Steps, a very similar technology for healing and restoration is set forth, a clear structure of accountability for knowing, speaking, and hearing the full truth, so it does not "kill" the addict or others. Perhaps that is the best kind of "retribution" and the only one that really helps both parties at the spiritual level.

A Direct Encounter With God's Love

When human beings "admit" to one another "the exact nature of their wrongs," we invariably have a human and humanizing encounter that deeply enriches both sides—and

even changes lives—often forever! It is no longer an exercise
to achieve moral purity, or regain God's love, but in fact a
direct encounter *with* God's love. It is not about punishing
one side but liberating both sides.

If you are still inside the economy of merit, which is a *quid
pro quo* universe, you will undoubtedly not like this, which is
why it has taken us so long to get here. The economy of grace
was exemplified in Desmond Tutu's "Truth and
Reconciliation Commission" in South Africa after the fall of
apartheid, where all had to take proper and public responsibility for their mistakes, not for the sake of any punishment
but for the sake of truth and healing. In fact, *the healing was
the baring—and the bearing—of the truth publicly.* This is revolutionary and unheard-of in human history but is actually totally
biblical, starting with the prophet Ezekiel during and after the
Exile, and dramatically lived out by Jesus.

Ezekiel laid the biblical groundwork for truth-speaking,
totally accountability, and restorative justice. For him, the
cement that holds the whole thing together is Yahweh being
true to Yahweh's Self, and not merely *reacting* to human
failure (or God would not be free, said Franciscan scholar
John Duns Scotus). For Ezekiel, God always acts with total
freedom, from divine integrity and unilateral faithfulness to
the covenant with Israel, whether they keep their side or not.
This becomes the foundational theme of radical grace,
without which "grace would not be grace at all" (Romans
11:6).

Speaking for Yahweh, Ezekiel says, "I treat you as respect for my own name requires and not as your own wicked behavior and corrupt actions deserve" (20:44). When Israel sins, and lies exposed like a naked whore, Yahweh only loves Israel more and at ever-deeper levels (16:1–63). Yahweh uses the word *restore* six times here to describe how he will "punish" Israel, their enemy Samaria, and their hated inferior Sodom. Here we have Yahweh beautifully loving and liberating all parties involved. Yahweh's "punishment" comes precisely by loving and forgiving them and keeping his side of the covenant forever, which reduces them to "shame, silence, and confusion" (16:63). (This morphed into the medieval notion of purgatory, by the way!)

I always felt Paul was making the very same point when he quoted Proverbs to say that you should give food and drink to those who are enemies, and "heap red hot coals on their head" (Romans 12:20). He is leading up to "resist evil and conquer it with good," which is the next line (12:21). Have you ever experienced the embarrassed and red-faced look of shame and self-recognition on the face of anyone who has been loved gratuitously after they have clearly done wrong? This is the way that God seduces us all into the economy of grace—by loving us in spite of ourselves in the very places where we cannot or will not or dare not love ourselves.

God resists our evil and conquers it with good, or how could God ask the same of us?! Think about that. God shocks and stuns us into love. *God does not love us if we change, God loves us so that we can change.* Only love effects true inner transformation, not duress, guilt, shunning, or social pressure. Love is not love unless it is totally free. Grace is not grace unless it is totally free. You would think Christian people would know that by now, but it is still a secret of the soul.

The usual and expected ego pattern is this:

sin —> punishment —> repentance —> transformation.

This is totally recalibrated by Ezekiel, after experiencing the perfection of Yahweh's love for Israel, which is always the purifying touchstone. For him the pattern is radically changed and becomes instead:

sin —> unconditional love —> transformation —> repentance

—with our now "embarrassed and humiliated face" being our ongoing punishment and conversion! Grace is always a punishment for us.

Ezekiel the prophet, through mounting and outrageous metaphors, first *disqualifies* Israel as worthy of any love by reason of their complete unfaithfulness, and then he completely *requalifies* them by reason of the totally one-sided "covenant love" of God! Whether it be the self-serving shepherds (chapter 34), the whoring girl (chapter 16), or the field of dry bones (chapter 37), in every case Yahweh *punishes* them by loving them even more! Yahweh says to Ezekiel, "I take no pleasure in the death of a wicked man, but in the turning back of a wicked man who changes his ways to win life. Come back, come back! Why are you so anxious to die, House of Israel?" (33:11) *Israel is, of course, the standing metaphor and symbol for the individual soul and all of history.* If this is indeed the pattern, as I believe it surely is, what hope it gives us all!

The Sacrament of Confession as One Accountability System

I would like to illustrate these two patterns of merit and grace by comparing the ecclesial sacrament of reconciliation with Step 5 of A.A.

Accountability and healing was so deemed necessary in the history of Christianity that it became an official and designated role in the community, and even a "Sacrament." Someone had to be trained and prepared for the dumping, ventilating, releasing, and absolving that humans always need. Someone had to be prepared to sit in the "mercy seat" (Exodus 25:17–22) and declare with authority that what God forgives, they dare not hold against themselves or one another. Our judgments are not greater than God's. When it is indeed a mercy seat, and not a juridical courtroom, people will be changed, often dramatically. Our tendency *to resist, doubt, and deny ourselves forgiveness* made it necessary for one person to speak and act with absolute authority for the sake of the soul: "I announce to you in the name of God, and with the authority of the Holy Spirit, that all of your sins are forgiven," the confessor might say. There often needs to be a human mirror to reflect the un-seeable divine gaze, especially if our heads and body are bowed in shame.

The official sacrament of reconciliation or "confession" was bound by the strictest rules of secrecy, and anonymity too if the penitent chose, so he or she would feel absolutely safe and able to be completely vulnerable. I have witnessed it myself from both sides, and know it can be a powerful liminal space for both penitent and confessor. Therapists have told me they would give anything to achieve the same trust and tenderness in a sometimes five-minute encounter. The power of the relationship allows you to do much healing in a short time—and much damage if you do not sit compassionately on the mercy seat. This is the special power of spiritual authority, and it is deeply needed at key turning points in our lives. Such Christians are blessed indeed!

The trouble is that we were not completely honest about how Jesus offered this gift of confession and accountability to his people. We seem to have relied on most Catholics' *non*-knowledge of the Bible here. The text quoted in the epigraph above that is normally the classic text to "prove" the priest's power to forgive sins was, in fact, addressed to the larger group called "the disciples" (John 20:19–20), and not specifically to the smaller group that were specifically called "the twelve." In other words, Jesus gave this gift and call to the whole community, and only later did it devolve to the needed role of a specific spiritual authority.

In fact, in studying the history of the sacrament of reconciliation, we find that it was for most of the early centuries a public event on a few special days, and only the bishop had the authority to declare to the whole community their penance and God's forgiveness. We would now call it "General Confession" and *what was once the norm is now usually forbidden*. It was rebellious Celtic monks, railed against by Rome, who took the role to themselves because the people needed the encounter to be one-on-one, available everywhere, and all the time.[1]

Ordinary people in times of shame and doubt needed an *anamchara*, or a "soul friend." Soon what was once condemned as a dangerous fad from the Irish became by the time of the Council of Trent, ending in 1563, the *only* way that sins could be forgiven, demanding private auricular confession of sins in number and kind, and whether you sinned "alone or with others." This became the regular norm for Catholics for almost five centuries. We limited the power of "binding and loosing" to a small group instead of teaching it to the whole group (Matthew 18:18). It probably reflects the level of consciousness at that time, which was more the "magical" level than our later "relational" and mutual level, as "Spiral Dynamics" studies reveal.

What was lost was a healing and forgiving community, where the hurts usually happened anyway, but could now be bypassed for a more vertical and very private notion of sin. Confession of sin became a largely cosmetic and attitudinal notion, except for the folks who committed occasional major offenses, but they rarely went to confession anyway. If God has only forgiven the sins of people who have gone to the

Catholic sacrament in proper form, then I think it is safe to say that 99.999% of human sin has remained unforgiven by God. That can't be true. In actual practice, Catholic confession became a pious devotional exercise and had little to do with the development of real conscience or societal maturity.

All notions of social sin, offenses against the common good, the family, the neighborhood, the rest of creation, or the future were all forgotten in favor of a few "hot" sins and an endless laundry list of trivia that we barely felt guilty about. Half of all confessions are about "missing Mass on Sunday." We used to say that hearing 90 percent of confessions was like being stoned to death with marshmallows! For the recipients, it was like a Saturday night shower, whereby we could seek moral purity much more than moral maturity. We encouraged *"according to form"* confessions and *"according to form"* absolutions, while many Catholics went about being pretty much as greedy, materialistic, enemy-hating, unfaithful, and warlike as everybody else.

This did not create strong peer relationships in the community or family, as Step 5 practices often do. We did an end run around the needed apologies, the daily admission of faults, and the request for forgiveness face-to-face, and went to an uninvolved third party. It was surely good and helpful in some cases, but it did not tend to heal or restore actual human relationships at any practical level.

Step 5 tried to remedy these deficiencies in its own honest and practical way. It returned confession to all three levels—

God, self, and at least one other human being. It returned the mystery of forgiveness to where Jesus first offered it—to *peer confession and peer counseling*. Yet Step 5 did not let anyone glide by too easily, but insisted on the sharing of "the exact nature of our wrongs." It thus restored some notion of peer accountability and personal responsibility for our mistakes and failures.

Restore Relationships, Integrity With Myself, and Communion With God

Step 5 is far from any notion of retributive justice, which the sacrament of "penance" too often became, and returned to the much more biblical notion of restorative justice—to restore relationships themselves, to restore integrity with myself, and to restore a sense of communion with God. "Say five Our Fathers and five Hail Marys as a penance" still perpetuated a de facto notion of a juridical exchange instead of any deep experience of healing forgiveness or unearned grace. You cannot deal with spiritual things in a courtroom manner. It does not achieve its purpose; it does not work at a deep level. We forgot our own unique job description as people of the Gospel and imitated courts of law instead. Too often we sat on judges' benches instead of the mercy seat from which Yahweh restored Israel to health.

What humanity needs is an honest exposure of the truth, and true accountability and responsibility for what has happened. Only then can human beings move ahead with dignity.

This method of "restorative justice" is now being used in some negotiations, conflicts, and prisons around the world, and could well change our very notion of justice, and bring it much closer to divine justice. One would hope that the church would be leading the way here, and indeed it was the Catholic Bishops' Conference of New Zealand who wrote a groundbreaking document in 1989 on this subject, called "Revenge or Reconciliation."

Yet some American bishops are back into excommunicating people right and left, but almost always on the Left, hoping retribution will change these terrible "liberal" Catholics. Studies now show that threat and punishment are the least effective forms of social change or long-lasting improvement. They are efficient yes, but not effective at all. We can prove this from numerous educational studies. One has to wonder, do we really want people to grow, or do we just want to be in control of the moment? I am not speaking just of bishops or priests, but of parents and civil authorities too.

Only mutual apology, healing, and forgiveness offer a sustainable future for humanity. Otherwise we are controlled by the past, individually and corporately. We all need to apologize, and we all need to forgive or this human project will surely self-destruct. No wonder that almost two-thirds of Jesus' teaching is directly or indirectly about forgiveness. Otherwise, history winds down into the taking of sides, deep bitterness, and remembered hurts, plus the violence that inevitably follows. As others have said, "Forgiveness is to let go of our hope for a different or better past." *It is what it is*, and such acceptance leads to great freedom, as long as there is also accountability and healing in the process.

Nothing new happens without apology and forgiveness. It is the divine technology for the regeneration of every age and every situation. The "unbound" ones are best prepared to unbind the rest of the world.

·

CHAPTER SIX

The Chicken or the Egg:
Which Comes First?

·

Were entirely ready to have God remove all of these defects of character.

—Step 6 of the Twelve Steps

·

"This is what I shall tell my heart, and so recover hope: the favors of Yahweh are not all passed, his kindnesses are not exhausted. They are renewed every morning."

—Lamentations 3:21–22

"Not that I have become perfect yet: I have not yet won, but I am still running to capture the prize for which Christ Jesus captured me."

—Philippians 3:12

"The only thing that counts is not what humans want or try to do, but the mercy of God."

—Romans 9:16

"If I will it? Of course I will it! Be healed."

—Jesus (Luke 5:12)

·

It was easy for me to find many bib-
lical quotes validating Step 6, and I could have used many
more, because this step, although not commonly followed, is
thoroughly biblical. It struggles with—and resolves—the old
paradox of the chicken and the egg. It first recognizes that we
have to work to see our many resistances, excuses, and block-
ages, but then we have to fully acknowledge that God alone
can do the "removing"! But which should come first, grace or
responsibility? The answer is that *both* come first.

All we can do is get out of the way and then the soul takes
its natural course. Grace is inherent to creation from the
beginning (Genesis 1:2), just like springtime; but it is a lot of
work to get out of the way and allow that grace to fully operate
and liberate. The dilemma is a constant one: Does the
chicken produce the egg, or does the egg produce the
chicken? Does God "produce" us, or do we by our efforts "produce" God? Which side do you come down on? It has been a
constant tension in theology and spirituality, although usually
a false one.

The seeming paradox was summed up in an old aphorism: *No one catches the wild ass by running after him, yet only those who run after the wild ass ever catch him.* If both Pope Leo X and Martin Luther had meditated on that line, we might have avoided the acrimony of the initial Protestant Reformation. The pope emphasized that we had to run and "work for our salvation in fear and trembling" (Philippians 2:12), while Luther held the more radical Gospel position of free grace and no one really needs to run at all. God's love is a totally free gift, as Paul taught (Romans 9:11–12, 11:6, and throughout). Both Luther and the pope were right and also both misunderstood and marginalized one another, which later Catholic–Lutheran dialogues now admit. We did not have much non-dual consciousness in those days, but we largely operated with what A.A. rightly calls "all or nothing" thinking, and which I call dualistic thinking.

Almost all true spirituality has a paradoxical character to it, which is why the totally rational or dualistic mind invariably misses the point, and just calls things it does not understand wrong, heresy, or stupid. G.K. Chesterton said that paradox is simply truth standing on its head to get our attention! Christians actually revel in paradoxes without even realizing it: Jesus is totally human and totally divine at the same time, God is both one and three at the same time, Mary is both virgin and mother at the same time, the bread is both wheat and Jesus at the same time. We gave people these doctrines to believe, and then did not give them the proper software to process those very beliefs, and so ended up producing far too many atheists and *former* Roman Catholics and Evangelicals.

Step 6 manages to again talk paradoxically. It says that we must first fully own and admit that we have "defects of character," but then equally, step back and do nothing about it, as it were, *until we are "entirely ready" to let God do the job!* This really shows high-level spiritual consciousness. The aggressive Catholics will love the part about acknowledging your defects of character, and the true Lutherans (not sure how many there are?) will step back and wait for grace! Step 6 is saying they are both right and they are both wrong.

I like to say that we must "undergo God." Yes, God is pure and free gift, but there is *a necessary undergoing* to surrender to this Momentous Encounter. As others have put it, and it works well in English, *to fully understand is always to stand under* and let things have their way with you. It is strangely a giving up of control to receive a free gift and find a new kind of "control." Try it and you will believe the paradox for yourself.

The connection point is perhaps clarified in a quote from photographer Ansel Adams who would wait days and hours for the perfect circumstances and ideal light to take his iconic photos. He said, *"Chance favors the prepared mind."* Any gifted person knows this to be true. They look like geniuses to the outsider, and they often are, but there is method behind their holy madness. They have learned to wait for and fully expect what Hungarian psychology professor Mihaly Csikszentmihalyi brilliantly calls "flow."[1] It is no surprise at all that our common metaphors for the Holy Spirit all honor and point to a kind of flow experience: living water, blowing wind, descending flames, and alighting doves.

So the waiting, the preparing of the mind for "chance," the softening of the heart, the deepening of expectation and desire, the "readiness" to really let go, the recognition that I really do not want to let go, the actual willingness to change is the work of weeks, months, and years of "fear and trembling." The pope was right, even if he did not always do it himself!

The Supreme Insight of the Gospels

But the recognition that it is finally "done unto me" is the supreme insight of the Gospels, which is here taught practically in Step 6. It is the same prayer of Mary at the beginning of her journey (Luke 1:38) and of Jesus at the end of his life (Luke 23:46): "Let it be done unto me!"

Luther was right, too, even if he did not always do it himself. His reassertion of what Paul clearly taught in Romans and Galatians was the more hidden and mysterious part of the equation, and the Christian world must ever thank Martin Luther for his courage and persistence in recovering Paul and the Gospel for the Western "can-do" world.

The only problem is that it devolved into our modern private and personal "decision for Jesus Christ as my Lord and Savior" vocabulary, without any real transformation of consciousness or social critique on the part of too many Christians. *Faith itself became a "good work" that I could perform,*

and the ego was back in charge. Such a mechanical notion of salvation frequently led to all the right religious words, without
much indication of self-critical or culturally critical behavior.
Usually, there was little removal of most "defects of character,"
and many Christians have remained thoroughly materialistic,
warlike, selfish, racist, sexist, and greedy for power and
money—while relying on "amazing grace" to snatch them into
heaven at the end. And it probably will! But they surely did
not bring much heaven onto this earth to help the rest of us,
nor did they speed up their own salvation into the present.
Many "born agains" have made Christianity laughable to
much of the world (I can't just pick on Catholics!).

I will keep this chapter short, so you can just struggle with the
paradox itself, hold the creative tension until you can see that
two seeming contraries might not be contrary at all. I suggest
that you find examples of how this has been true in your own
life, and surely in any journey toward sobriety. It is always true:
We must both try and not try, we must both "care and not care,"
as poet T.S. Eliot puts it. We named our whole work after this
dilemma: "The Center for Action and Contemplation." It
seems we must both surrender and take responsibility.

By personal temperament you will start on one side or the
other, but finally you must build the bridge between the
two—and let it be built for you—both at the same time. Or
to reverse an old aphorism: We must *pray as if it all depends on
us, and work as if it all depends on God* (yes, you read that
correctly!).

If you caught the wild ass, it was by running and not running at the same time. Both the chicken and the egg forever produce one another and only dualistic thinking creates the dilemma. Grace will always favor the prepared mind. Maybe we can sum it up this way: God is humble and never comes if not first invited, but God will find some clever way to *get* invited.

CHAPTER SEVEN

Why Do We Need to Ask?

•

Humbly asked [God] to remove our shortcomings.

—Step 7 of the Twelve Steps

•

"Have mercy on me, O God, in your goodness, in your great tenderness wipe away all my faults, wash me clean of my guilt, and purify me from all my sin."

—Psalm 51:1–2

"If there is anything you need, pray for it, asking God for it with thanksgiving; and the peace of God, which is much greater than understanding, will guard both your thoughts and your heart."

—Philippians 4:6–7

"In your prayers do not babble on as the pagans do, for they think that by using many words they will make themselves heard. Do not be like them; your Father knows what you need even before you ask him."

—Matthew 6:7–8

•

Well, if God already knows what we need before we ask, and God actually cares about us more than we care about ourselves, then why do both Step 7 and Jesus say, each in their own way: "Ask, and you will receive. Seek, and you will find. Knock, and the door will be opened" (Matthew 7:7)? Are we trying to talk God into things? Does the group with the most and the best prayers win? Is prayer of petition just another way to get what we want? Or is it to get God on our side? In every case, notice that *we* are trying to take control.

In this short chapter I will simply try to address that one simple, often confused, but important mystery of *asking*. Why is it good to ask, and what is really happening in prayers of petition or intercession? Are we needed or encouraged to talk God into things? Why does Jesus both tell us to ask and then say, "Your Father already knows what you need, so do not babble on like the pagans do" (Matthew 6:7)?

Let me answer in a few brief sentences, and then I will backtrack and attempt to explain what I mean. *We ask not to change God but to change ourselves. We pray to form a living relationship, not to get things done.* Prayer is a symbiotic relationship with life and with God, *a synergy which creates a result larger than the exchange itself.* (That is why Jesus says all prayers are answered, which does not appear to be true according to the evidence!) God knows that *we* need to pray to keep the symbiotic relationship moving and growing. Prayer is not a way to try to control God, or even to get what we want. As Jesus says in Luke's Gospel the answer to every prayer is one, the same, and the best: the Holy Spirit! (See 11:13.) God gives us power more than answers.

Keeps Us From Entitlement

The death of any relationship with anybody is to have a sense of *entitlement.* Any notion that "I deserve," "I am owed," "I have a right to," "I am higher than you" absolutely undermines any notion of faith, hope, or love between the involved parties. This is certainly why Jesus made one of his strongest statements found in all three Synoptic Gospels, and yet one of his most denied and ignored. He says, "It is easier for a camel to pass through the eye of a needle than for a rich man to enter the kingdom of God" (Luke 18:25). Jesus says that about no other group. The mind of a rich person is invariably one of entitlement. "I deserve this because I worked hard for this!" we think. Or, "I am owed this by reason of my station in life" as even many clergy or famous people have imagined (with full cooperation and codependency from the crowds, I must add).

To undo and undercut this arrogant and soul-destructive attitude, Jesus told us all to stay in the position of a beggar, a petitioner, a radical dependent, which is always spiritually true, if we are honest. To know that you don't know, to know that you are always in need, to know you are a "nomad and stranger on this earth" (Hebrews 11:14) as my father Francis quoted in our Rule, keeps you situated in a place of structural truth. Let me explain.

Beggars Before God and the Universe

The longer I live the more I believe that truth is not an abstraction or an idea that can be put into formulas or mere words. Our *real truth has to do with how we situate ourselves in this world.* Josef Pieper, a German Catholic philosopher, said many years ago that "the natural habitat for truth is in interpersonal relationships," whereas we have made truth an idea on paper. There are ways of living and relating that are honest and sustainable and fair, and there are utterly dishonest ways of living and relating to life. This is our real, de facto, and operative "truth," no matter whose theories or theologies we believe. Our life situation and our style of relating to others is "the truth" that we actually take with us to the grave. It is who we are, more than our theories about this or that. Jesus says as much in his parable of the two sons. (See Matthew 21:28–32.)

Prayers of intercession or petition are one way of situating your life with total honesty and structural truth. It is no accident that both the early Franciscans and many Buddhist monks were official mendicants or beggars. Francis and Buddha did not want us to lose this central message, which is now almost entirely lost in our self-made, can-do, and climbing culture. What has been lost is honest relationship with the earth and with one another, and a basic humility too. *How you do life is your real and final truth,* not what ideas you believe. We are all and forever beggars before God and the universe.

We can never engineer or guide our own transformation or conversion. If we try, it will be a self-centered and well-controlled version of conversion, with most of my preferences and addictions still fully in place but now well disguised. Any attempts at self-conversion would be like an active alcoholic trying to determine his own rules for sobriety. God has to radically change the central reference point of our lives. We do not even know where to look for another reference point because up to now it has all been about me! Too much "me" can never find "you"—or anything beyond itself.

So Step 7 says that we must "humbly ask God to remove our shortcomings." Don't dare go after your faults yourselves or you will go after the wrong thing, or more commonly a clever substitute for the real thing. "If you try to pull out the weeds, you might pull out the wheat along with it," as Jesus says (Matthew 13:29).

Instead you have to let God (1) reveal your real faults to you (usually by failing and falling many times!), and then (2) allow God to remove those faults from his side and in God's way. If you go after them with an angry stick, you will soon be left with just an angry stick—and the same faults at a deeper level of disguise and denial. Thus most early-stage people in alcoholic recovery just replace one addiction with another: Now it is nicotine, caffeine, stinkin' thinkin', and the angry stick, which is now OK because it is a Christian angry stick.

God's totally positive and lasting way of removing our short-comings is to fill up the hole with something much better, more luminous, and more satisfying. Then your old short-comings are not driven away, or pushed underground, as much as they are *exposed and starved* for the false program for happiness that they are. Like used scaffolding, our sins fall away from us as unneeded and unhelpful because now a new and better building has been found. This is the wondrous dis-covery of our True Self, and the gradual deterioration of our false and constructed self.[1]

When you learn what good food is, you are simply no longer attracted to junk food. You don't need to crusade against greasy burgers and fries, you just ignore them. They become uninteresting as you happily search out the whole, organic, fresh, and healthy markets. *All spiritual rewards are inherent and not rewards that are given later.* Take that as a trustworthy axiom. Not heaven later as much as health now—which prepares you for—and becomes—heaven later!

Right Relationship With Life Itself

Gerald May, a dear and now deceased friend of mine, said in his very wise book *Addiction and Grace* that *addiction uses up our spiritual desire.* It drains away our deepest and true desire, that inner flow and life force which makes us "long and pant for running streams" (Psalm 42). Spiritual desire is the drive that God put in us from the beginning, for total satisfaction, for home, for heaven, for divine union, and it just got displaced onto the wrong object. It has been a frequent experience of mine to find that *many people in recovery often have a unique and very acute spiritual sense;* more than most people, I would say. It just got frustrated early and aimed in a wrong direction. Wild need and desire took off before boundaries, strong identity, impulse control, and deep God experience were in place.[2]

So it is important that you ask, seek, and knock to keep yourself in right relationship with Life Itself. Life is a gift, totally given to you without cost, every day of it, and every part of it. A daily and chosen "attitude of gratitude" will keep your hands open to expect that life, allow that life, and receive life at ever-deeper levels of satisfaction—but never to think you deserve it. Those who live with such open and humble hands receive life's "gifts, full measure, pressed down, shaken together, and running over into their lap" (Luke 6:38). In my experience, if you are not radically grateful every day, resentment always takes over. *For some reason, to ask "for your daily bread" is to know that it is being given.* To not ask is to take your own efforts, needs, and goals—and yourself—far too seriously. Consider if that is not true in your own life.

After a few years in recovery, you will know that your deep and insatiable desiring came from God all along, you went on a bit of detour, looked for love in all the wrong places, and now have found what you really wanted anyway. God is willing to wait for that. Like Jacob at the foot of his dreamy ladder, where angels walk between heaven and earth, you will lay your head on even a stone pillow, and say, "You were here all the time, and I never knew it! This is nothing less than the house of God, this is the very gate of heaven" (Genesis 28:16–17).

It's even better than that. The final discovery, as Thomas Merton put it, is that this "gate of heaven is everywhere"! Now all of our faults and ego possessions are just heavy and burdensome luggage that keep us from walking through this always-open gate—or even seeing it in the first place.

CHAPTER EIGHT

Payback Time

Made a list of all persons we had harmed, and became willing to make amends to them all.

—Step 8 of the Twelve Steps

•

"Nathan said to David, 'You are the man!'. . . And David said to Nathan, "I have indeed sinned."

—2 Samuel 12:7, 13

"In judging others you condemn yourself, since you behave no differently than those you judge."

—Romans 2:1

"If you are bringing your gift to the altar, and there remember that your brother or sister has anything against you, go first and be reconciled to him or her, and then come back and present your gift."

—Matthew 5:23–24

•

Despite the higher economy of grace and mercy lived and taught by Jesus, he did not entirely throw out the lower economy of merit or "satisfaction." They build on one another, and the lower just finds itself inadequate to the truly great tasks of life—love, forgiveness, unjust suffering, and death itself. The universal principle is called "transcend and include." When you move to higher states of love and transformation, you do not jump over the earlier stages but must go back and rectify the earlier wrongs, or there will be no healing or open future for you—or for those you have hurt.

God fully forgives us, but the "karma" of our mistakes remains, and we must still go back and repair the bonds that we have broken. Otherwise others will not be able to forgive us, will remain stuck, and we will both remain a wounded world. We usually need to make amends to forgive even ourselves. Edward Tick, in his important book *War and the Soul,* illustrates that one of the most effective healings for some soldiers with post-traumatic stress disorder (PTSD) was to go back to Vietnam and work for orphans and the handicapped. Otherwise, *they* were never free.

"Amazing grace" is not a way to avoid honest human relationships, but to redo them—but now gracefully—for the liberation of both sides. Nothing just goes away in the spiritual world; all must be reconciled and accounted for. All healers are *wounded healers*, as Henri Nouwen said so well. There is no other kind. In fact, you are often most gifted to heal others precisely where you yourself were wounded, or wounded others. "We are only the earthenware jars that hold this treasure, to make it clear that such overwhelming [healing] power comes from God and not from us" (1 Corinthians 4:7). You are being prepared to be a healer (which will be Step 12).

You learn to salve the wounds of others by knowing and remembering *how much it hurts to hurt*. Often this memory comes from the realization of your past smallness and immaturity, your selfishness, your false victimhood, and your cruel victimization of others. It is often painful to recall or admit, yet this is also the grace of lamenting and grieving over how we have hurt others. We have found at our conferences that safely constructed "liturgies of lamentation" can be very fruitful for social and personal change. Fortunately, God reveals our sins to us gradually so we can absorb what we have done over time. "Little by little you correct those who have offended you, so that they can abstain from evil, and learn to trust in you, O God," says the book of Wisdom (12:2).

Our family, friends, and enemies, however, are not as kind or patient as God. They need a clear accounting to be free and go ahead with their lives. Often they just need to talk it through, hear our understanding, and maybe our sincere apology. Usually they need to offer their understanding of the situation and how it hurt them. *Neither side needs to accuse or defend, but just state the facts as we remember them, and be open to hear what the other needed, heard, or felt.* It has developed into a true art form, and some rightly call it "redemptive listening" or "nonviolent communication."[1] Knowing we were not taught nonviolent communication at the personal level, is it any surprise that we did not have the skills at the national, cultural, or church levels?

It is no surprise that history has been nonstop wars and violence. We have not developed much capacity for redemptive listening or "fighting fair," but now we are rebuilding society from the bottom up as honest communication skills are now being taught to married couples, families, therapists, prisoners, and educators. I now see life coaches and martial arts instructors teach nonviolence more directly and more effectively than most Sunday sermons or religious education classes, which tend to proceed from dualistic thinking. Things are so different than what we once expected.

So Step 8 is quite programmed, concrete, and specific. "Make a list," it says, and that list is of "all those *we* have harmed." Note that it does not say those who have harmed *us*, which will just get us back into the self-serving victim role. The plan is absolutely inspired here, and knows that it needs to push the addict out of his or her immense selfishness. A.A. is the only group I know that is willing and honest enough to just tell people up front, "You are damn selfish!" Or, "Until you get beyond your massive narcissism you are never going to grow up." They are just like Jesus who told us without any hesitation that we had to "renounce ourselves" (Mark 8:34) to go on the path. Most of us still do not believe that, much less like it.

Almost all other groups avoid this balance in one direction or the other. Liberal and sophisticated groups are usually trapped in current social correctness, and just keep affirming peoples' selfishness. It is classic enabling and codependency, with too much false horizontal affirmation and almost no vertical truth-speaking. Most fundamentalist and conservative groups just threaten people with God's harsh judgment and their own, but do not normally teach people how to heal or how to make amends, or how to let go in practical, emotional, and mental ways (no teaching of contemplation). "Jesus has forgiven it, so we can forget about it." This is far too vertical with almost no horizontal dimension. Their guilt problem was solved and that is all that matters. *It is a self-serving concern to alleviate just your own guilt; it is a loving question to say, "How can I free others from theirs?"*

The Geometry of the Cross

Even the geometry of the cross should tell us that we need both dimensions, the vertical and the horizontal. We are the religion of "incarnation" (enfleshment or embodiment) not spiritualization. Once the Eternal Blueprint ("Logos") became flesh, it is in the material world that we find God. Incarnation is our major trump card (John 1:14)! Step 8 is a marvelous tool and technology for very practical incarnation, which keeps Christianity grounded, honest, and focused on saving others instead of just ourselves. "Anyone who claims to be in the light, but hates his brother or sister, is still in the dark" (1 John 2:9). Until religion becomes flesh, it is merely Platonic idealism instead of Jesus radicalism.

The second bit of spiritual genius in Step 8 is that it recognizes how long it might take to be truly "willing." It even uses the active verb "*became willing* to make amends to them all" to help us see that it is always *a process* and must finally include all. To offer an apology in a way that can actually heal the other takes wisdom and respect for the other.

Did you ever have someone apologize to you and it felt much more like the person just wanted to let you know how wonderful and Christian they were to forgive you? They are normally trying to regain their bruised self-image by thinking of themselves as magnanimous. It sometimes takes the form of a very properly said, "I forgive you, but I hate your sin." There could perhaps be a good way to understand that statement, but it usually means, "I am on moral high ground, but you are not." The person unlocks himself or herself but not the other person. Christians love to say this to gay people, exonerating and exalting themselves, while binding up the other, and not even knowing it.

I remember saying to an employee once, "I accept your forgiveness, but why is it that I do not *feel* forgiven?" We were both still "held bound" by his attempt to free himself without also freeing me. Jesus gave us all the wonderful power to both lock and unlock reality. It does not work if we just try to unlock ourselves but do not also unlock the other person. This is another classic example of the Roman Church presuming we did *not* know Scripture. It always quotes Matthew 16:19 where the power of "binding and loosing" is given to Peter and never points out that two chapters later in Matthew 18:18, Jesus says the same thing to the whole community, and now even introduces it by an "I tell you solemnly." This might be called selective or preferential memory, whereas the true Gospel is always "dangerous memory."

Willing to Make Amends

At any rate, we all need to do some clean-up work inside. For humans, there is only a slow softening of the heart, a gradual lessening of our attachment to our hurts, our victimhood as a past identity, or any need to punish or humiliate others. "'Vengeance is mine,' says the Lord" (Romans 12:19). Vengeance against the self or vengeance against anything is not our job. It might take a long time to "become willing" to make amends, and that is why some people go to Step 8 meetings for years.

They learn to make lists, but not of what others have done to them, which is the normal ego style, and a pattern once practiced that is very hard to stop. Instead they have been given some new software, a program called *grace*, a new pattern, a "new mind" (Ephesians 4:23; Colossians 3:10–11; 1 Corinthians 2:16), a new processing system. Instead of making lists of who hurt me, I now make lists of people *I* have perhaps hurt, failed, or mistreated, and then do something about it. It might be a note, a call, a visit, a meaningful gift, an invitation, an outright apology. God will show you the best way, the best place, the best time, and the best words. Wait and pray for them all.

Remember once again Einstein's brilliant idea that no problem can be solved by the same consciousness that caused the problem in the first place. Making such a list will change your foundational consciousness from one of feeding resentments to a mind that is both grateful and humble—all the time.

•

•

CHAPTER NINE

Skillful Means

•

Made direct amends to such people wherever possible, except when to do so would injure them or others.

—Step 9 of the Twelve Steps

•

"Like apples of gold in a silver setting is a word that is aptly spoken. It is a golden ring, an ornament of finest gold, such is a wise apology to an attentive ear."

—Proverbs 25:11–12

"To listen to the word and not obey it is like looking at your own features in a mirror and then, after a quick look, going off and immediately forgetting what you look like."

—James 1:23

"Father, I have sinned against heaven and against you. I no longer deserve to be called your son, treat me as one of your paid servants."

—Luke 15:19

•

What the Western religions some-times called "wisdom," the Eastern religions often called "skillful means." Wisdom was not a mere aphorism in the head, but a practical, best, and effective way to get the job done! One was either trained in skillful means by a master or parent, or it would be the long laborious school of trial and error, which seems to be the unfortunate pattern today. I am afraid that commonsense wisdom, or skillful means, is no longer common sense. We are a culture with many elderly people but not so many elders passing on wisdom.

Jesus was a master of teaching skillful means, especially in his Sermon on the Mount, and in many of his parables and one-liners. But we got so preoccupied with needing to prove and worship Jesus' divinity that we failed to let him also be a sage, a wise man, a teacher of commonsense spiritual wisdom. We just waited for another dogmatic declaration to fall from his lips—about how he was God—which he seemingly never made—instead of hearing his daily and constant declarations about how to be human and how we were to imitate him in his humanity.

He proudly and most often called himself a "son of man," emphasizing what we have been afraid to emphasize. Jesus' by far most common name for himself, imitating the prophet Ezekiel (who uses it ninety-nine times), was "a son of humanity," one of you, the archetypal human, everyman.[1] It is almost his only name for himself, and never "I am the Son of God." He even tells the disciples *not* to tell people that he is the Christ!. (See Matthew 16:20.) It seems to be another example of selective memory because it is so amazing that we tried to tie the "Son of Man" title up with one obscure passage in Daniel 7:13, with a capitalization that would not have existed in the original. But that kept the Gospel properly "otherworldly," and we could all imagine its possible connotations while ignoring its clear denotation. In fact, its meaning was just what it said, "I am a classic human being" and one of you! We kept Jesus out of the range of actual imitation, when the very goal was to imitate him in his combined humanity and divinity. Remember, Jesus said "follow me" and never once said "worship me." The sad result is that we have many "spiritual" beings when the much more needed task is to learn how to be true human beings. Full humanness leads to spirituality by the truckload, or as the Scholastic theologians said, "grace builds on nature" and cannot do an end run to heaven.

So you might say that Step 9 is telling us how to use skillful means to both protect our own humanity and to liberate the humanity of others. It also says that our amends to others should be "direct," that is, specific, personal, and concrete, in other words, probably not an e-mail or a tweet. Jesus invariably physically touched people and met people when he healed them. It is face-to-face encounters, although usually difficult after a hurt, that do the most good in the long run, even if the other party rebuffs you at the first attempt. You opened the door from your side, and it thus remains open, unless *you* reclose it.

But the most skillful insight is the cleverly added "except when to do so would injure them or others." Bill W could only have learned such wisdom by doing it wrong, probably many times. It takes seven to ten years, they say, for a married couple to begin to learn how to fight fairly. One often needs time, discernment, and good advice from others before one knows *the when, how, who, and where* to apologize or make amends. If not done skillfully, an apology can actually make the problem and the hurt worse, and the Twelve Steps were experienced enough to know that. Not everything needs to be told to everybody, all the time, and in full detail. Sometimes it only increases the hurt, the problem, and the person's inability to forgive. This all takes wise discernment and often sought-out advice from others.

Anonymity and Total Disclosure

We have a myth of "total disclosure" in our culture that is not always fair or even helpful. Just because it is factually true, does not mean everyone can handle it or even needs to handle it, or has a right to the information. You need to pray and discern about *what the other needs to hear and also has the right to hear.* What people *want* to hear in salacious and gossipy detail has now been fed by our media-saturated society, and our wanting to know has become our right to know. Gossip is not a right but a major obstacle to human love and spiritual wisdom. Paul lists it equally with the much more grievous "hot sins" (Romans 1:29–31), and yet most of us do it rather easily.

In training us for our work as confessors, a wise Franciscan told us that we should not, and in fact it was wrong of us to, "demand a manifestation of conscience" from another person. Some things are not everybody's business—not even the confessor's. Any prying or undue questioning had more to do with our own morbid curiosity than any love for the healing or helping of the other person. We would do well to teach this to our whole society to protect one another from slander, rash judgment, and ill will. Is this not part of why the word "anonymous" is in the very A.A. title?

Finally, something about truth, truth-telling, and deceit: Truth is not just "what happened" but also *what you or any party has a right to know—and can handle responsibly.* For an addict, a gay person, a person with a preexisting physical ailment, there are people who have a right to that knowledge, and frankly people for whom it is none of their business, and people who will misuse it. Even our government recognized this in what we call the Fifth Amendment, stating that people have the right not to incriminate themselves. To say to an unwelcome guest at the door, "No, Mother is not home," might be factually a lie, but in fact it might be very true on a level that could deeply matter: "Mother is not home for you"! In confessional work, we called it a "mental reservation," and it was sometimes not just good but, in fact, the more moral thing to do to protect yourself or others, or even the party seeking the information. "Not everybody has a right to know everything" is a moral principle that our culture would be wise to learn.

Skillful means is not just to make amends but to make amends in ways that "do not injure others." Truth is not just factual truth (the great mistake of fundamentalists), but a combination of both text and context, style and intent. Our supposed right to know every "truth" about our neighbor too often feeds those with preexisting malice, bias, or mental imbalance, and leads to spin, distortion, and misinterpretation of supposed facts. I have met many falsely accused people in jails and in treatment homes, accused by the court of public opinion, with information that was totally manipulated by angry politicians or tabloid forms of journalism. It has become its own form of pornography and is just as destructive to the soul, to basic justice, and to peoples' right to their own good name.

The Twelve Steps are about two things: making amends and keeping us from wounding one another further. Too much earnest zeal here, "spilling the beans" on everybody's lap, will usually create a whole new set of problems. Many people simply do not have the proper "filters" to know how to process ideas or information; they often misuse them without intending to misuse them. Even sincere people can do a lot of damage with information that they are not prepared to handle, and often make rash judgments that are not true or helpful. It is likely what St. Teresa of Avila was referring to when she said, "Lord, protect me from such saints!" Step 9 does just that.

CHAPTER TEN

Is This Overkill?

Continued to take personal inventory and when we were wrong promptly admitted it.

—Step 10 of the Twelve Steps

•

"But who can detect his own failings? Who can expose his own hidden faults?"

—Psalm 19:12

"Even pagans who never heard of the law, can be said to 'be' the law; it is engraved on their hearts. They can call forth this witness, their own inner mental dialogue of accusation and defense."

—Romans 2:14–15

"Then Jesus said to him a third time, 'Simon, son of John, do you love me?' Peter was upset that he asked him a third time, and said, 'Lord, you know everything, you know that I love you.'"

—John 21:17

•

I must admit when I first read Step 10, I wanted to say, "OK, come now, let's get on to something a bit more positive and evolved. This is beginning to feel like an endless examination of conscience, and will keep people navel-gazing forever." I still recognize that as a danger for some. I do believe our religious history has been too guilt-based and shame-based, and not enough of what some would call "vision logic," which is a broader, positive, and out-in-front kind of motivation. Jesus' metaphor and draw was a positive vision he called "the kingdom of God," which he seemed to be constantly talking about. For Bill W it was a "vital spiritual experience." Neither of these were *a negative threat, but a positive allure, promise, and invitation.* For me, this is crucial and necessary or the spiritual journey largely becomes fear-based problem-solving.

I come from a religious life practice where we learned from the Jesuits about a daily and personal "examination of *conscience"* which certainly had some wise intent and worked for some. But I found that people with a mature conscience did this naturally anyway, and some way too much. Now many of the Jesuits recommend instead an "examination of *consciousness*," which to me feels much more fruitful. I guess that is what I would recommend if I were teaching Step 10, and also because it transitions well into Step 11 on prayer and meditation. So let's talk about consciousness a bit.

Consciousness as Soul Itself

Consciousness is the subtle and all-embracing mystery within and between Everything. It is like the air we breathe, take for granted, and do not appreciate. Consciousness is not the seeing but *that which sees me seeing*. It is not the knower but *that which knows that I am knowing*. It is not the observer but *that which underlies and observes me observing*. You must step back from your compulsiveness, and your attachment to yourself, to be truly conscious. Consciousness cannot be "just me" because it can watch "me" from a distance. Author and psychologist Ken Wilber describes it beautifully as "the simple feeling of Being" underneath all of our perceptions, and yet so simple and subtle and always there that it is hard to "feel," I would add. Consciousness is as hard to describe as *soul* is hard to describe. Maybe because they are same thing?

Consciousness is *aware of* my feelings so it cannot be purely and simply *my* feelings themselves. Who or what is that awareness? Most people do not get that because they are rather totally identified with their own thoughts, feelings, and compulsive patterns of perception. You see why so many of our mystics and saints emphasized detachment so much. Without it, people could not move to the soul level. Meister Eckhart said detachment was the whole deal, and the early Franciscans seemed to talk about nothing else, though they called it "poverty." We do not live in a culture that much appreciates detachment or such poverty. We are consumers by training and habit, which is exactly why we have such problems with addiction to begin with! For properly detached persons (read "nonaddicted"), deeper consciousness comes rather naturally. *They discover their own soul—which is their deepest self—and yet has access to a Larger Knowing beyond themselves.* This is one description of our mysterious and multifaceted soul. We would have done better to help people *awaken* this soul rather than trying to save it (often unawakened!) for the next world.

If "obeyed," yes, *obeyed*, consciousness will become a very wise teacher of soul wisdom and will teach us from deep within (Jeremiah 31:33, and Romans 2:15, both called it "the law written on our hearts"). Some call it the "Inner Witness" and this witness is what Christians have called the Holy Spirit, which has hovered over creation since the Big Bang (Genesis 1:2), that is, the first moment when God began to materialize. Fourteen-and-a-half billion years after the Big Bang, or the cosmic incarnation, when humanity was ready for conscious encounter, this same Spirit hovers over a single Jewish girl, Mary, to effect and reveal what we Christians would call the *human* incarnation in Jesus (Luke 1:35). Biblical scholar Walter Brueggemann calls it "the scandal of the particular."

Just as it has been equally hard for us to believe in our own Spirit-filled incarnation as children of God (see Romans 5:5, 8:9–10), it has been hard for many to believe that Jesus could be God's "child" too. Jesus is not an exclusive son of God, however, but the inclusive son of God, revealing what is always true everywhere and all the time. Paul resolves this subtlety, by calling us "adopted" sons (Galatians 4:5) and "co-heirs with Christ" (Romans 8:17).

So, on one level soul, consciousness, and the Holy Spirit can well be thought of as the same thing, and it is always larger than me, shared, and even eternal. That's what Jesus means when he speaks of "giving" us the Spirit or *sharing his conscious-ness with us.* One whose soul is thus awakened, actually has "the mind of Christ" (1 Corinthians 2:10–16). That does not mean the person is psychologically or morally perfect, but such transformed people do henceforth see things in a much more expanded and compassionate way. Ephesians calls it "a spiritual revolution of the mind" (4:23). And it is!

Jesus calls this implanted Spirit the "Advocate" (John 14:16) who is "with you and in you" (14:17), who makes you live with the same life that he lives (14:19), and unites you to every-thing else (14:18, 20). He goes on to say that this "Spirit of truth" will "teach you everything" (14:26) and "remind" you of all you need to know (14:26). Talk about being well equipped for life from a Secret Inner Source! It really is too good to believe—and so we didn't.

This loss and sadness led me one Lent to write sixty-five names for this hidden mystery in a "Litany of the Holy Spirit."[1] It was really my homage to a Loving Inner Consciousness that we all share, but we have not been taught to rely upon or to allow to guide us. Most churches gave people the impression they would "get" the Holy Spirit as a reward for good behavior, in occasional dire circumstances, if they were writing a Gospel, or when a bishop would lay his hands on them. We severely limited the Spirit's available working hours, and edged God's defending Presence out of its pivotal role for us. We were left "orphaned," exactly what Jesus said he did not want (14:18). Maybe the old German-based word "Holy Ghost" (*geist*) was a correct premonition of what had happened or not happened. The Holy Spirit had become an invisible ghost or mind.

Consciousness, our soul, the Holy Spirit, on both the individual and the shared levels, has sadly become *unconscious*! No wonder we call the Holy Spirit the "missing person of the Blessed Trinity." No wonder we try to fill this *radical disconnectedness* by various addictions. There is much evidence that so-called "primitive" people were more in touch with this inner Spirit than many of us are. British philosopher and poet Owen Barfield called it "original participation" and many ancient peoples seemed to have lived in daily connection with the soulful level of everything—trees, air, the elements, animals, the earth itself, along with the sun, moon, and stars. These were all "brother" and sister" just as St. Francis would later name them. Everything had "soul" and spirituality could be taken seriously and even came naturally. Most of us no longer enjoy this consciousness in our world. It is a "disenchanted" and lonely universe for most of us. We even speak of the "collective unconscious," which now takes on a whole new meaning. We really are disconnected from one another and thereby unconscious. Yet, religion's main job is to reconnect us (*re-ligio*) to the Whole, to ourselves, and to one another—and thus heal us. We have not been doing our job very well.

Our Divine Identity as Children of God

So a daily "examination of *consciousness*" sounds like a very good thing indeed. Paul wisely makes this point of an inner knower in several subtle passages that show real insight; he calls it "the mind of Christ" and the "inner law" (see 1 Corinthians 2:10–16 and Romans 2:14–15), which seems to be an inherent sharing in this one Spirit or consciousness. In another place he speaks of both ourselves and God, carrying a "united witness" (Romans 8:16) to our divine identity—as "children of God," "heirs," and "coheirs with Christ" (8:17).[2] When we stopped trusting this inner and united witness, we had no support in believing the central Gospel message itself—that *we share in the same identity as Jesus* (1 John 3:1–2; 2 Peter 1:4). That should be more than enough to heal anyone of their low self-esteem, insecurity, or the addictions that we all use to fill this tragic void.

Wisely, Step 10 does not emphasize a *moral* inventory, which becomes too self-absorbed and self-critical, but it speaks of a "personal inventory." In other words, *just watch yourself objectively, calmly, and compassionately.* You will be able to do this from your new viewing platform and perspective as a grounded child of God. "The Spirit will help you in your weakness" (Romans 8:26). From this most positive and dignified position you *can* let go of, and even easily "admit your wrongs." You are being held so strongly and so deeply that you can stop holding onto, or defending, yourself. God forever sees and loves Christ in you; it is only *we* who doubt our divine identity as children of God.

We now have an implanted position and power whereby we can see ourselves calmly and compassionately without endless digging, labeling, judging, or the rancor that we usually have toward our own imperfection. *Don't judge, just look* can be our motto—*and now with the very eyes of God.* That will awaken consciousness, and then things will usually take care of themselves, with even the least bit of honesty and courage. A wonderful Indian Jesuit, Anthony de Mello, used to say, "Awareness, awareness, awareness!" Once we see our inherent dignity clearly, the game of evil and addiction begins to collapse. Evil always relies upon camouflage to have its way. Evil must get us to doubt our inherent dignity, just as in Jesus' temptations in the desert, where Satan precedes each temptation with the same line, "If you are the son of God" (Matthew 4: 3, 6). Once we doubt that, we will slip into addiction and the unconscious, and we will easily do evil—and not even call it evil. When we are standing in our inherent dignity, we can easily do Step 10, calmly taking "the personal inventory," and then having the security to "promptly admit it when we are wrong." People who know *who they are* find it the easiest to know *who they aren't.*

Whenever we do anything stupid, cruel, evil, or destructive to ourselves or others, we are at that moment *unconscious,* and unconscious of our identity. If we were fully conscious, we would never do it. Loving people are always highly conscious people. To rely on any drug or substance is to become unconscious. I always find it sad in counseling when people share that they have to have some wine or alcohol to *make love* to their wife or husband. In a very real way that is a contradiction in terms because we cannot actually be loving when we are unaware or not fully present.

To be fully conscious would be *to love everything* on some level and in some way—even our mistakes. To love is to fall into full consciousness, which is contemplative, non-dualistic, and including everything—even "the last enemy to be destroyed, which is death itself" (1 Corinthians 15:26). That is why we must, absolutely must, *love!*

Didn't Jesus tell us that we must love even our enemies? When we can on some level even love our sins and imperfections, which are our "enemies," we are fully conscious and fully liberated. God, who is Universal Consciousness itself, knows all things, absorbs all things, and forgives all things—for being what they are. *If Jesus commands us to love our enemies, then we know that God must and will do the same.* What hope and joy that gives us all! It takes away all fear of admitting our wrongs.

> Yes, you love all that exists,
> you hold nothing of what you have made in abhorrence,
> for had you hated anything, you would not have formed it.
>
> And how, had you not willed it, would a thing persist in being?
> How could it be conserved if not called forth by You?
> You spare all things, because all things are yours,
> Lord, lover of life, you whose imperishable spirit is in all.
>
> —Wisdom 11:25—12:1

—————————— CHAPTER ELEVEN ——————————

An Alternative Mind

•

Sought through prayer and meditation to improve our conscious contact with God, *as we understood [God],* **praying only for knowledge of [God's] will for us and the power to carry that out.**

—*Step 11 of the Twelve Steps*

•

"Be still, and know that I am God."

—*Psalm 46:10*

"You must put aside your old self which has been corrupted by following illusory desires. Your mind must be renewed by a spiritual revolution."

—*Ephesians 4:22–23*

"In the morning, long before dawn, he got up, left the house, and went off to a lonely place to pray."

—*Mark 1:35*

•

Let me tell you something very important, and something that Step 11 was able to recognize quite well. The word *prayer,* which Bill Wilson rightly juxtaposes with the word *meditation,* is a code word for *an entirely different way of processing life.* When you "pray," you are supposed to take off one "thinking cap" and put on another "thinking cap" that will move you from an egocentric perspective to a soul-centric perspective. Although it is not really "thinking" at all, but what Canadian writer Malcolm Gladwell calls the genius of "thinking without thinking."

I call the first perspective "the calculating mind," and I call the second perspective "the contemplative mind."[1] These are two entirely different types of software, and since the first one is almost totally and always in control, and has become your only operative hardware, you have to be *carefully taught* how to pray, which is exactly what the disciples asked of Jesus, "Lord, teach us how to pray" (Luke 11:1). If you do not learn how to pray, and change "your mind…by a spiritual revolution," as Ephesians says above, you will try to process the big five human issues (love, death, suffering, God, and infinity) with utterly inadequate software. It won't get you very far.

Because we have not been teaching people how to switch this receiver station, we are producing a lot of neurotic and angry behavior as people cannot deal with these central issues. One has to go through some initial withdrawal pains to switch processors, and this is why prayer takes some initial "work" to learn how to do that. Once Western people can get rid of any prejudices against Buddhism, they must be honest enough to admit that true Buddhists tend to be much more disciplined and honest about this switching of "thinking caps."

The first mind sees everything through the lens of its own private needs and hurts, angers, and memories. It is too small a lens to see truthfully or wisely or deeply. I am sure you know that most people do not see things as they *are*, they see things as *they* are! Take that as a given. So most spiritual traditions and religions taught prayer in some form; but at its truest, it was always an alternative processing system. For many, if not most, Christian believers, however, it became a pious practice or exercise that you carried out with the same old mind and from your usual self-centered position. This practice was supposed to "please" God somehow. God needed us to talk to Him or Her, I guess. Prayer was something you did when you otherwise felt helpless, but it was not actually *a positive widening of your lens for a better picture*, which is the whole point.

Being Willing to Let God Change You

In what is commonly called prayer, you and your hurts, needs, and perspectives are still the central reference point, but now you have decided to invite a Major Power in to help you with your already determined solution. God can help you get what you want, which is still a self-centered desire, instead of God's much better role—which is to *help you know what you really desire* (Luke 11:13; Matthew 7:11). It always takes a bit of time to widen the lens, and therefore the screen, of life. One goes through serious withdrawal pains for a while until the screen is widened to a high-definition screen. It is work to learn how to pray, largely the work of *emptying the mind and filling the heart.* That is all of prayer in one concise and truthful phrase!

At early-stage praying, there has usually been no real "renouncing" of the small and passing self (Mark 8:34), so it is not yet the infinite prayer of the Great Body of Christ, but the very finite prayer of a small "body" that is trying to win, succeed, and take control—with a little help from a Friend. God cannot directly answer such prayers, because frankly, *they are usually for the wrong thing and from the wrong self,* although we do not know that yet.

In short, prayer is not about changing God, but being willing to let God change us, or as Step 11 says, "praying only for the knowledge of his will." Jesus goes so far as to say that true prayer is *always* answered (Matthew 7:7–11). Now we all know that is not factually true—unless he is talking about prayer in the sense that I am trying to describe it. *If you are able to switch minds to the mind of Christ, your prayer has already been answered! That new mind knows, understands, accepts, and sees correctly, widely, and wisely. Its prayers are always answered because they are, in fact, the prayers of God too.*

True prayer is always about getting the "who" right. Who is doing the praying? You or God in you? Little you or the Christ Consciousness? The contemplative mind prays from a different sense of Who–I–am. It rests, and abides in the Great *I AM*, and draws its life from the Larger Vine (John 15:4–5), the Deeper Well (John 4:10–14). Paul puts it this way: "You are hidden with Christ in God. When Christ is revealed—and he is your life—you too will be revealed in all your glory within him" (Colossians 3:3–4). It does not get any better than that, and you are now personally in on the deal. Basically prayer is an exercise in *divine participation*—you opting in and God always there!

So you see why it is so important to "pray," that is, to change your "thinking cap," because it largely has to do with how your mind processes things, and then the heart and body will normally come along. The mind is the normal control tower, so it must be educated first. Even rational-emotive therapy has come to recognize this is true. Most practices of meditation and contemplation have to do with *some concrete practices to recognize and to relativize the obsessive nature of the human mind. The small mind cannot deal with Bigness and Newness, which God always is!* Even most addiction counselors recognize that many addicts are "all or nothing thinkers." I call this dualistic thinking, and is the normal labeling, rational mind that is good for things like science, math, and turning left or right. But it is at a complete loss with the big five of God, death, suffering, love, and infinity.

But do not think I am trying to give a mere secular or psychological meaning to prayer. Not at all. Why would I waste your time? Jesus himself gives very similar advice when he says things like, "When you pray, go to your inner room, and shut the door." Knowing there was no such thing as an "inner room" in a Jewish one-room house, they would have known that he was talking about the inner self, what we would now called the unconscious, your personal inner room, as it were. This is also indicated by his double use of the word *secret* as both a place where the truth is waiting unawares and a place hidden to most of us—in which God "dwells" and from which God "blesses" (Matthew 6:6).

Shortly after this, Jesus also says, "When you pray, do not babble on like the pagans do," which is pointing to something other than mere verbal prayer. I would call it *the prayer of quiet*. In fact, the very fact that the disciples have to ask him for a verbal prayer could well make the case that he had not taught them one! Groups usually had their public, group prayer to define their identities, much like the Serenity Prayer of A.A. Jesus' disciples said, "John the Baptist taught his disciples a prayer, we want one too" (Luke 11:1), and one could conclude that what we call the Our Father was in part a concession, probably a good one, to that understandable social need of ours.

But let's be honest, *Jesus himself goes into silence, into nature, and usually alone when he prays.* (Check it out in Luke 3:21, 5:16, 6:12, 9:18, 28–29, 11:1, and 22:41.) It is rather amazing we have not noted this. With our emphasis on Sunday social prayer and liturgical prayer and prayer meetings, this might again be an example of selective and preferential memory. Since the thirteenth century, no one has been teaching us what to do with our minds when we were alone, at least in any systematic way.[2] So Sunday morning singing, reading, and recitation of group prayers took over, even though they were much less evident in the life of Jesus.

It is the prayer of quiet and self-surrender that will best allow us to follow Step 11, which Bill W must have recognized by also using the word *meditation* when that word was not common in Christian circles at all at that time. And he was right, because only contemplative prayer or meditation invades, touches, and heals the *unconscious!* This is where all the garbage lies—but also where God hides and reveals "in that secret place" (Matthew 6:6). "Do you not know," Jesus says, "the kingdom of God is *within you!*" (Luke 17:21).

Most other forms of prayer have too many external forms and too much social payoff and thus keep us in the calculative mind. I know this from years in religious community and parishes where we have public prayers every day, and yet many people's motivations and goals still mirror the larger world. So Jesus wisely says, "When you pray, don't imitate those who love to say their prayers standing up in the synagogue or at street corners for people to see them. They have already received their reward" (Matthew 6:5). Again, it is amazing this had so little effect on Christian forms of prayer. I guess we thought standing up in synagogues was bad, but standing up in churches was good?

For most of two chapters in Matthew (6 and 7), Jesus warns us against the unconscious social payoffs in all public encounters: prayer, fasting, almsgiving, clothing, money, class systems, social judgments, and possessions. These all keep people from going to any deep level and facing their real issues. We must admit that Christian cultures have not been appreciably different than others in these regards. Maybe we could say *lex orandi est lex vivendi*, "how you pray determines how you finally live." How you first live inside is how you will deal with things outside. If prayer itself is largely an external performance of any kind, there is simply *no* inner life to keep us honest and real and grounded.

Jesus himself "went off by himself" (Mark 1:35) to pray, which takes a lot more courage, choice, and trust than mere attendance at a service. I am sure he participated in appropriate temple and synagogue services, although it is hardly mentioned in the Gospels. It does say he read and taught in the synagogue, which is a bit different than prayer (see, e.g., Luke 4:16, 31–32). Perhaps we can see the limitations of an overemphasis on social prayer better in other world religions; many do it more regularly and rigorously than Christians do, but can also remain at very low levels of real change of behavior. Perhaps this is revealed in the first demon encounter in Luke's and Mark's Gospel—it is in the synagogue itself! (Mark 1:23–24). Yes, there is such a thing as addiction to religion, and there has been much written about it in recent years that is quite helpful.[3] Religion can also be its own kind of demon. What better place to hide?

Social prayer can hold the group together, but it does not necessarily heal the heart or soul of the group—often the opposite, as it unites them against a common foe or heresy. On TV recently I saw Muslim men coming directly from pious prayer in the mosque to hatefully waving their fists against their enemies. I know too many Christian clergy who have celebrated liturgies much of their lives and are still infantile, spiritually speaking. You do too. "It is what comes out of a person that makes him or her unclean. For it is within, from people's *hearts* (their word for the unconscious) that evil *intentions* emerge and make a person unclean" (Mark 7:21), so we must have a form of prayer that changes us from the inside. Intentionality and real motivation are not some new psychological self-help idea. Jesus called it "the inside of cup and dish" as opposed to our preoccupation with "the outside of cup and dish" (Matthew 23:25–26). Jesus tried to move history toward interiority whenever possible, and it has been a long slog.

Conscious Contact With God

The Twelve Step Program was quite ahead of its time in recognizing that we need forms of prayer and meditation that would lead us to "conscious contact with God," beyond mere repetition of correct titles and names and formulas, which religions fight about ("God as we understand God."). Such a Step 11 can lead us to real inner "knowledge of his will for us" (instead of just external commandments for all), and for the "power to carry it out" (actual inner empowerment and new motivation from a deeper Source). How can anyone say the Twelve Steps are not deeply inspired?

The fruits of prayer and meditation are so evident that the only way I got into Folsom and San Quentin prisons was to teach Step 11. The local authorities said that this new quiet prayer seemed to actually "change people," even people on death row or in for life. For years, I was a part of "competing" church services at the local Albuquerque jail, where each group divided over externals of worship style, denominational histories, and vocabulary. When we did contemplative or "centering prayer" together, however, most of those divisions meant nothing, even who was leading the service was unimportant. There was no room for fighting over clergy, gender, or ordination; only competence and authenticity mattered.[4]

Let me end this chapter with a fine quote from Thomas Merton who said: "The will of God is not a 'fate' to which we must submit, but a creative act in our life that produces something absolutely new, something hitherto unforeseen by the laws and established patterns. Our cooperation consists not solely in conforming to external laws, but in opening our wills to this mutually creative act."[5]

It is such divine *synergy*, people's willingness to creatively work with the hand that life and sin and circumstance and God have dealt them that is our deepest life of prayer and devotion. This is "doing the will of God"! We are still afraid and unfamiliar with such calm inner authority, the "law written our hearts" promised by Jeremiah (31:33), until we set out on an actual journey of "prayer and meditation." Until then, religion is largely externals and formulas, about which we fight or divide. I hope this chapter sends you on such a journey of "conscious contact," where there is nothing to fight about and only much to enjoy.

People's willingness to find God in their own struggle with life—*and let it change them*—is their deepest and truest obedience to God's eternal will. We must admit this is what all of us do anyway, as "God comes to us disguised as our life"! Remember, always remember, that *the heartfelt desire to do the will of God is, in fact, the truest will of God*. At that point, God has won, and the ego has lost, and your prayer has already been answered.

Let's sum up the importance of an alternative mind in this fine message from an unknown source:

Watch your thoughts; they become words.
Watch your words; they become actions.
Watch your actions; they become habits.
Watch your habits; they become character.
Watch your character; it becomes your destiny.

—————————— CHAPTER TWELVE ——————————

What Comes Around Must Go Around

•

Having had a spiritual awakening as a result of these steps, we tried to carry this message to alcoholics, and to practice these principles in all our affairs.

—Step 12 of the Twelve Steps

•

"You have cured me and given me life, my suffering has turned to health. It is you who have kept my soul from the pit of nothingness, you have thrust all my sins behind your back! The living, the living are the ones who praise you, as I do today."

—Isaiah 38:16–17, 19

"What we have heard and known for ourselves must not be withheld from our descendents, but be handed on by us to the next generation."

—Psalm 78:3–4

"Simon, Simon, you must be sifted like wheat, and once you have recovered, you in your turn must strengthen your brothers."

—Luke 22:31–32

"What was given to you freely, you must give away freely."

—Matthew 10:8

•

After trying to teach the Gospel for over forty years, trying to build communities, and attempting to raise up elders and leaders, I am convinced that one of my major failures was that I did not ask more of people from the very beginning. If they did not turn outward early, they tended never to turn outward, and their dominant concern became personal self-development, spiritual consumerism, church as "more attendance" at things, or to use the common phrase used among Christians "deepening my relationship with Jesus" (most of which demands little accountability for what you say that relationship is). Bill W seemed to recognize this danger early on.

Until people's basic egocentricity is radically exposed, revealed for what it is, and foundationally redirected, much religion becomes occupied with rearranging deck chairs on a titanic cruise ship, cruising with isolated passengers, each maintaining his or her personal program for happiness, while the whole ship is sinking. I am afraid Bill Plotkin, psychologist and agent of cultural transformation, is truthful and fair when he says that we live in a "patho adolescent" culture.[1] One of the few groups that name that phenomenon unapologetically is Alcoholics Anonymous. Read, for example, page 62 of the *Big Book:* "So our troubles are basically of our own making. They arise out of ourselves; and the alcoholic is an extreme example of self-will run riot, though he or she does not think so. Above everything, we alcoholics must be rid of this selfishness. We must, or it kills us!" What courage it took him to talk this way.

Why can't we all be that honest—and therefore truly helpful? Well, Step 12 found a way to expose and transform that pathological adolescence by telling us early on that we must serve others. It is not an option, not something we might eventually be "called" to after thirty-five religious retreats and fifty years of church services; it is not something we do when we get our act together. No, we do not truly comprehend any spiritual thing until we ourselves give it away. Spiritual gifts increase only by "using" them, whereas material gifts normally decrease by usage.

It is a karmic law of in and out, and what Jesus really meant when he sent the disciples out "to cast out devils, and to cure all kinds of diseases and sickness" (Matthew 10:1) or to "Go out to the world and proclaim the Gospel to all creation" (Mark 16:16). He knew we had to hand the message over before we really understood it or could appreciate it ourselves. Over forty years as a preacher myself, I have no doubt that it has been my attempts to preach, teach, and counsel others that have re-convinced and partially converted me!

Jesus was not talking about forming a new in-group, but transmitting a message that actually made a difference for people and for human society. As Tradition Eleven of A.A. will say, "Our public relations policy is based on attraction rather than promotion." If it really heals, they will come, A.A. believes; whereas much of organized religion says in effect, "Come join our group, and maybe we will get to some actual healing some day." Francis McNutt, trained in the Dominican "Order of Preachers," calls it "the nearly perfect crime": Although Jesus spent all of his ministry moving between preaching and healing, with the healing validating the preaching, most of church history has done loads of preaching and very little healing.[2] *Seminaries are set up to train teachers and preachers, not healers.*

We would have done well to take seriously that most neglected Letter of James, which Luther called "the epistle of straw." I personally believe that James, perhaps written by a brother of Jesus, or at least a head of the Jerusalem church, represents the more primitive message. At that point in our history, we have more *lifestyle Christianity* than doctrinal theories. James always insists on orthopraxy instead of mere verbal orthodoxy: "To listen to the word and not obey it is like looking at your own features in a mirror, and then, after a quick look, going off and immediately forgetting what you look like" (1:23–24). For James, to "actively put it into practice is to be happy in all that one does" (1:25), and, "If good works do not accompany faith, it is quite dead" (2:14). James is a unique apostle of the Twelve Step behavioral approach.

What makes me or anybody think that we really believe in Jesus, much less follow him, unless we somehow pass it on "to the least of the brothers and sisters" (Matthew 25:40) as he commanded? It is the spiritual equivalent of the First Law of Thermodynamics: *Energy cannot really be created or destroyed, it is merely converted to different uses.* What comes around *must* go around, or it does not come around again.

Inhalation and Exhalation

A person will suffocate if she just keeps breathing in, which might be exactly what has happened. The Jewish name for the Holy One, literally unspeakable, is "Yahweh," which we now believe was an imitation of the sound of breathing in and breathing out.[3] It could not be uttered but only breathed. The sacred name of God (Exodus 3:14) is already revealing the deepest pattern of all reality, which is the cycle of taking in and giving back out. It is the shape of all creation, which Christians called a Trinitarian circle of indwelling and out-pouring, and was the very shape of God and of all reality formed in God's image.[4] It is all there, like a cosmic hidden code, at the very beginning and foundation of our Traditions.

I know of a fine priest who established a most amazing and effective parish in New York State. He told me that when new members would come to join, he would at the very first meeting say, "And for what service group can I sign you up?" It was an absolute condition of membership. No passive attendance was allowed there, and he would not accept any excuses either. I think of most Catholic parishes, where there are a group of stalwarts who come to Mass every day, hear a daily sermon, and for whom we turn on the lights and heat up the church. A recent study said that these are not the same people who do most of the ministry or volunteer work in those same churches. They just "attend" their daily spiritual event. Without realizing it, we are training them in taking and training them in *not giving*. No wonder we largely descended into mere civil religion and cultural Catholicism, with so many passive members.

A.A. would call this *enabling unhealthy codependency*, and there are special meetings just for such a sickness—for those who foster it, allow it, and profit from it. It is called Al-Anon. We must learn to distinguish between what looks like loving and what is actually loving for such codependent members of our churches. A.A. recognized that most people need tough love or they do not grow beyond their inherent selfishness. Passive membership creates not just passive dependency but also far too often passive-aggressive behavior—when such stalwart members do not get what they have become accustomed to. Every pastor knows what I am talking about. Many arch-conservative Catholics are great lovers of the papacy, until the pope talks about the evils of war, capitalism, capital punishment, or the rights of labor unions (In fact, they often refuse to admit that he even said such things!). That is the predictable passive-aggressive behavior you can expect when there has been no actual spiritual awakening.

"Having Had a Spiritual Awakening"

We now return to where it should all start—the necessity of "a vital spiritual experience," or what Step 12 calls a spiritual awakening. It is the grand plan and program for human deliverance. Yes, God could have created us already awakened, but then we would have been mere robots or clones. If God has revealed anything about who God is, then it is enormously clear that *God loves and respects freedom—to the final and full and riskiest degree.* God lets evil take its course, and does not even stop Hitler or people who torture children. We will look at this more in the final chapter.

A good spirituality achieves two huge things simultaneously: It keeps God absolutely free, and not bound by any of our formulas, and it keeps *us* utterly free ourselves and not forced or constrained by any circumstances whatsoever, even human laws, sin, limitations, failure, or tragedy. "It was for freedom that Christ has set us free!" as Paul says (Galatians 5:1). *Good religion keeps God free for people and keeps people free for God.* You cannot improve on that.

Believe me, it is a full-time job. Jesus spent much of his time defending his healing ministry from observant religious authorities, and reminded them that "the Sabbath was made for humanity, not humanity for the Sabbath" (Mark 2:27). We all seem to bind up both God and one another inside of our explanations, our preferences, and even our theologies. The patterns never seem to change.

When these two great freedoms meet, we have a spiritual awakening! And the world opens up beneath our feet and above our heads. We are in a differently shaped universe. It is not that God chooses some people to have a spiritual awakening, and others not. *Awakening just happens, as certain as the dawn, when the two great freedoms meet.* But keeping God free (from bad teaching, fear, and doubt) and getting you free (from selfishness, victimhood, and childhood wounds) is the big rub and the lifelong task. Like two super magnets, when the two freedoms are achieved simultaneously—even for a millisecond—they grab onto one another—and, as in nuclear fusion, an explosion always results. It is without doubt *the change that changes everything.* It is both divine lovemaking and human ecstasy.

For Bill Wilson, there is no real or long-lasting recovery, no real sobriety, much less "emotional sobriety," without what he calls a "vital spiritual experience." In the second appendix to the *Big Book,* he distinguishes between his own frequent use of the terms "spiritual awakening" and "vital spiritual experience." He rightly clarifies that most awakenings are not "in the nature of a sudden and spectacular upheaval," although even that is not infrequent. But usually, they are of the "educational variety because they develop slowly over a period of time." One gradually "realizes that he [*sic*] has undergone a profound alteration in his reaction to life, and that such a change could hardly have been brought about by himself alone." Nor could it "have been accomplished by years of self-discipline." As usual, he is both helpful and brilliant here.

I was counseling a young married man recently, and he was very discouraged with himself. No matter what, he could not stop being irritated at others, biting off people's heads, resenting every little thing. He said in desperation and anguish, "How can I change this? I don't know how to be different!" He sounded like Paul: "What a wretched man I am! Who will deliver me from this body of death?" (Romans 7:24). Then I asked him if he was that way with his two little children, and without any hesitation he said, "No, not at all, hardly ever."

You see the point, I am sure. The only way to be delivered from our "body of death" is *a love that is greater*, a deeper connection that absorbs all the negativity and irritation with life and with ourselves. Until we have found our own ground and connection to the Whole, we are all unsettled and grouchy. That man's children do that for him, as children often do for men, and that is what a vital spiritual experience does for you too. Afterward, you know you belong, you are being held by some Larger Force, and for some illogical reason life feels OK and even good and right. You are glad to be aboard the ship called Life—every day and all the time.

Do you know why most of us are called to marriage, and even "saved" by marriage and children, even marriages that do not last forever? *Marriage and parenting is made to order to steal you from your selfishness.* It first of all reveals your selfishness to you (The first seven years after the honeymoon, I am told, are not easy.), and then if you stay in there, and fall into *a love that is greater*, it is usually much easier from there. Not without work, however, because the ego and the shadow do not "go gentle into that good night," as Dylan Thomas would say.

Again and again, you must choose to fall into *a love that is greater* with both friends and children. It is all training for the falling into The Love that is the Greatest. All loves are a school of love, and their own kind of vital spiritual experience—until a lasting Relationship with the Real finally takes over. You learn how to "fall in love" by falling many times, and you learn from many fallings how also to recover from the falling. How else would you? But best of all, you only know what love is by falling into it, almost against your will, because it is too scary and too big to be searched out, manufactured, or even imagined ahead of time. Love, like God, "is a harsh and dreadful thing," according to Russian writer Fyodor Dostoyevsky. I wonder if that is why we both want but also avoid a vital spiritual experience?

Step 12 is saying something very risky, but very true, when it says that we will have this spiritual awakening "as the result of these steps." Bill W knows well that we cannot program grace and mercy, so why does he put it this way? It is not that we create or earn the spiritual awakening by our inner work; and yet without the work of falling and letting go, it does not seem to happen. The two freedoms do not meet one another. I suspect Bill W knew that we were "Yankee-can-do" Americans, and we needed a program to get us going. He also knew we would know only afterward that it was all grace anyway.

A Spiritual Disease

Let me end by pointing out that addiction has been described as a moral weakness, as a simple lack of willpower, a cowardly inability to face life, and also a spiritual illness or disease. I, of course, strongly believe that it is the latter. Addiction is a spiritual disease, a disease of the soul, an illness resulting from longing, frustrated desire, and deep dissatisfaction—which is ironically the necessary beginning of any spiritual path.

The reason that A.A. has been more successful than most churches in actually changing people and helping people is that it treats addiction both *spiritually and as an illness*, rather than as a moral failure or an issue of mere willpower. We in the churches tend to treat everything in terms of personal culpability, which only elicits immense push-back and the passive-aggressive response that I mentioned earlier. A.A. says, in its own inspired way, that addicts are souls searching for love in all the wrong places, but still searching for love. Alcoholism is deeply frustrated desire, as are all addictions. The Twelve Step Program has learned over time that addiction emerges out of *a lack of inner experience of intimacy with oneself, with God, with life, and with the moment.* I would drink myself to oblivion too, or look for some way to connect with solid reality, if I felt that bereft of love, esteem, joy, or communion.

One helpful clarification is that many addicts tend to confuse *intensity with intimacy,* just as most young people do with noise, artificial highs, and overstimulation of any sort. Manufactured intensity and true intimacy are complete opposites. In the search for intimacy, the addict takes a false turn, hopefully a detour, and relates to an object, a substance, an event, or a repetitive anything (shopping, thinking, blaming, abusing, eating) in a way that will not and cannot work for them. Over time, the addict is forced to "up the ante" when the fix does not work. *You need more and more of anything that does not work.* If something is really working for you, then less and less will satisfy you. On my good days, a grasshopper can convert me.

Good and nutritious food needs no fancy sauces, pretentious art gives way to the simple lines and textures of nature, quiet music satisfies deeply, a loving touch on the arm is better than a false orgasm, and after fasting, just a little bit of food gives one a jolt, a new sensation, and a sense that "it never tasted so good before!" When I return from my lenten hermitage of under-stimulation, it takes very little to totally delight me. It seems like everything has been painted with rich and fresh colors. The addict has actually denied himself this joy, a happiness that is everywhere and always, a simple feeling of being and being alive, when our very feet connect lovingly with the ground beneath us, and our head and hair with the undeserved air.

Addicts develop a love and trust relationship with a substance or compulsion of some kind, which becomes their primary emotional relationship with life itself. This is a god who cannot save. It is momentary intensity passing for the intimacy they really want, and it is always quickly over.

I am told that in the Hebrew Bible there is really only one sin, and the one and only sin is *idolatry*: making something a god that is not God. As the psalmist cleverly puts it, these idols "have mouths but speak not, eyes but see not, ears that hear not, noses that smell not, hands that do not touch, feet that will not walk. *And their makers end up like them, and everyone who relies on them*" (Psalm 115:5–8). There it is, with the same kind of blatant honesty that characterizes the Twelve Step Program. So, all of us, consumers, compulsives, and unconscious alike, don't waste any more time or worship on gods that cannot save us. We were made to breathe the Air that always surrounds us, feeds us, and fills us. Some call it God.

With these twelve important breathing lessons, you now know for yourself that you can breathe, and even breathe under water. Because the breath of God is everywhere.

•

•

Only a Suffering God Can Save

•

Who among those who have read the Gospels does not know that Christ makes all human suffering his own?

—*Origen, On Prayer[1]*

•

Theodicy is a branch of theology that has developed many arguments on how there can be a God, a good God, or a just God in the presence of so much evil in the world—about which "God" appears to do nothing, except an individual "change of heart" here and there? Especially when such changed hearts have not been in control of most of history, even in the churches.

The evidence is overwhelming that God fully allows and does not stop genocides, the abuse of children, brutal wars, unspeakable human and animal suffering, the imprisonment of the innocent, the sexual enslavement of girls, the regular death of whole species and civilizations, the tragic lives of addicts and their codependents. Further, God seems to fully "cause," or at least allow, the "natural" disasters of drought, flood, hurricane, tornado, tsunami, plague, infestation, physical handicap, mental illness, and painful disease of every kind, many of which we call "acts of God," and all of which have made much of human life "solitary, poor, nasty, brutish, and short."[2] What are we to do with this?

At my level of observation, any belief in a *deus ex machina* God, who jumps in to correct and improve things, any "god of the gaps" who quickly fills in for our ignorance and evil, is not what I see. Any "omnipotent God" who actually operates omnipotently is clearly not the pattern, and that is after years of thinking I have to run to God's defense, as if God needed me! I do not see any all-powerful God taking power at all. It is very disappointing on most levels, and frankly boggles the rational mind, if that is what a rational mind expects from the Divine. There has to be a better framing of both the question and any possible answer. Exactly *how* is God loving and sustaining what God created? That is our dilemma.

For me, there is a workable and loving way through this. If God is somehow *in* the suffering, participating as a suffering object too, in full solidarity with the world that He or She created, then I can make some possible and initial sense of God and this creation. Then I stop complaining long enough to sit stunned and awakened by the very possibility. At least if *we are participating in something together,* and human suffering has some kind of direction or cosmic meaning, I can forgive such a God for leaving us in what seems like such desperate straits, and maybe I can even find love and trust for such a God.

Only if we are not alone in this universe, can we tolerate our aloneness. Only if there is a bigger and better outcome, can we calm down and begin to listen and look. *Only if human suffering is first of all and last of all divine suffering can we begin to connect any dots.* Only if we are joining God, and God is joining us, in something greater than the sum of all its parts, can we find a way through all of this. I do know a number of individuals for whom this act of trust was enough to keep their heads high and their hearts open, even in hell. Trust in the cruci-fied—and resurrected—Jesus has indeed "saved" many.

I personally don't know how any of the contrived arguments of theology and theodicy finally help or convince anyone, except for those who have met the one Christians call *a cruci-fied God.* The rest just have to split or deny. Many of the happiest and most peaceful people I know love a God who walks with crucified people, and thus *reveals and "redeems" their plight as his own.* For them, Jesus is not observing human suffering from a distance but is somehow *in* human suffering with us and for us. He includes our suffering in the co-redemption of the world, as "all creation groans in one great act of giving birth" (Romans 8:22). Is this possible? Could it be true that we "make up in our own bodies all that still has to be undergone for the sake of the Whole Body" (Colossians 1:24)? Are we somehow business partners with the divine?

Is this the way that we matter? Is this the price of our inclu-sion inside of the Great Mystery that God has lived first and foremost? Is God truly and forever a Great Outpouring, as the Trinitarian pattern seems to say? When I see animals and plants and even the stars die so willingly and offer their bodies for another generation, or another species, or the illumina-tion of the universe, I begin to see the one pattern every-where. It is the truest level of love, as each and every thing offers itself for another. Would any of us even learn to love at all if it was not demanded of us, taken from us, and called forth by human tears and earthly tragedy? Is suffering necessary to teach us how to love and care for one another? I really believe that it is—by observation!

What Breathing Under Water Might Really Be

If you see where this "logic" is going, I am indeed saying that *only people who have suffered in some way can save one another*— exactly as the Twelve Step Program discovered. *Deep communion and dear compassion is formed much more by shared pain than by shared pleasure.* I do not know why that is true. We are not saved by any formulas or theologies or any priesthood extraneous to the human journey itself. "Peter, you must be ground like wheat, and once you have recovered, then you can turn and help the brothers" (Luke 22:31–32), Jesus says to Peter. Was that his real ordination to ministry? No other is ever mentioned. I do believe this is the only ordination that matters and transforms the world. Properly ordained priests might help bread and wine to know what it is, but truly ordained priests help people to know *who they are*, as they "help the brothers (and sisters)."

Only those who have tried to breathe under water know how important breathing really is, and will never take it for granted again. They are the ones who do not take shipwreck or drowning lightly, they are the ones who can name "healing" correctly, they are the ones who know what they have been saved *from*, and the only ones who develop the patience and humility to ask the right questions of God and of themselves.

You see, *only the survivors know the full terror of the passage, the arms that held them through it all, and the power of the obstacles that were overcome.* All they can do is thank God they made it through! For all the rest of us it is mere speculation, salvation theories, and "theology."

Theirs are no longer the premature requests for mere physical healing, or pure medical cures, as the lepers and the blind in the Gospels first imagined. Those who have passed over are now inside a much Bigger Picture. They know they are still and forever alcoholics, but something better has been revealed—and given to them—in the very process of passing over, which they can alone know from the other side. Only after the second laying on of Jesus' hands could the blind man at Bethsaida say, "Now I can see clearly, plainly, and distinctly" and know that he "was cured" (Mark 8:25). There is the first laying on of hands where "people look like trees walking around" (8:24), which might symbolize the initial stage of recovery from the mere physical addiction. The full emotional, spiritual, and relational illumination only comes with time, when we can see "clearly, plainly, and distinctly." The second healing is the more important one.

Those who have passed over eventually find a much bigger world of *endurance, meaning, hope, self-esteem, deeper and true desire, but most especially, a bottomless pool of love both within and without.* Their treasure hunt is over, and they are home, and home free! The Eastern fathers of the church called this transformation *theosis,* or the process of the divinization of the human person. This deep transformation is not achieved by magic or miracles or priestcraft but by a "vital spiritual experience" that is available to all human beings. It leads to an emotional sobriety, an immense freedom, a natural compassion, and a sense of divine union that is the deepest and most universal meaning of that much-used word *salvation.* Only those who have passed over know the real meaning of that word—and that it is not just a word at all.

It is at precisely this point that the suffering God and a suffering soul can meet. It is at this point that human suffering makes spiritual sense, not to the rational mind, the logical mind, or even the "just and fair" mind, but to the logic of the soul, which I would state in this way:

Suffering people can love and trust a suffering God,

Only a suffering God can "save" suffering people,

Those who have passed across this chasm can and will save one another.

Any other god becomes a guilty bystander, and one that you will not deeply trust, much less love. Christians should not, however, insist that "my Higher Power is better than your Higher Power." This is love of self and not love of God. But it is still good for Christians to know that their Jesus was *made to order* for the transformative problems of addiction and human suffering. From the cross, he draws all suffering people to himself.

What humiliated and wounded addict cannot look on the image of the crucified Jesus and see himself or herself? Who would not rush toward surrender and communion with such a crucified God, who against all expectations, shares in our powerlessness, our failure, and our indignity? Who would not find himself *revealed, renamed, and released* inside of such a God? As theologian Sebastian Moore said many years ago in a book of the same name, "the crucified Jesus is no stranger." Jesus is no stranger to history, no stranger to the soul, no stranger to any who have suffered—but a stranger to all others—even to many Christians. Jesus is more than anything else *the God of all who suffer*—more than any tribal god that can be encompassed in a single religion. Jesus is in competition with no world religion, but only in nonstop competition with death, suffering, and the tragic sense of life itself. That is the only battle that he wants to win. He wins by including it all inside of his body, "groaning in one great act of giving birth... waiting until our bodies are fully set free" (Romans 8:22–23). Finally, I have an answer!

The Awful Grace of God

The suffering creatures of this world have a Being who does not judge or condemn them, or in any way stand aloof from their plight, but a Being who hangs with them and flows through them, and even toward them in their despair. How utterly different from all the greedy and bloodthirsty gods of most of world history! What else could save the world? What else would the human heart love and desire? And further, this God wants to love and be loved rather than be served (John 15:15). How wonderful is that?! It turns the history of religion on its head.

Jesus said it of himself: "When I am lifted up from the earth, I will draw all people to myself" (John 12:32) and "from my breast will flow fountains of living water" (7:38). It is only the "harsh and dreadful" commingling of both divine love and human tears which opens the deepest floodgates of both God and the soul, and eventually I must believe, it will open history itself. I will sink my anchor here.

To mourn for one is to mourn for all. To mourn *with* all is to fully participate at the very foundation of Being Itself. For some reason, which I have yet to understand, *beauty hurts.* Suffering opens the channel through which all of Life flows and by which all creation breathes, and I still do not know why. Yet it is somehow beautiful, even if it is a sad and tragic beauty.

So let me end with the wisdom of a Greek dramatist, which should be another proof that the same Holy Spirit has been guiding all of history. Aeschylus, the Greek dramatist who lived from 525 to 456 BC, was not really *before Christ* at all, but already presents the one eternal message in concise and poetic verse. It is wisdom available to all of us, at least by our later years—and if we are listening:

He who learns must suffer.
And even in our sleep pain that cannot forget,
Falls drop by drop upon the heart,
And in our own despair, against our own will,
Comes wisdom to us, by the awful grace of God.[3]

•

———————— NOTES ————————

•

INTRODUCTION

1. Jose Ortega y Gasset available at http://www.philosophicalsociety.com/Philosophy2/Thoughts%20On%20Life-2.htm.

2. Thomas of Celano, "Second Life of St. Francis," *St. Francis of Assisi: Omnibus of Sources* (Cincinnati: St. Anthony Messenger Press, 2009), p. 208.

3. Unpublished poem quoted in *Inherited Illusions: Integrating the Sacred and the Secular* by Thomas Cullinan (Westminster, Md.: Christian Classics, 1988), pp. 56–57.

4. Tertullian, *De Resurrectione Carnis*, 8:2.

5. Richard Rohr, *Falling Upward: A Spirituality for the Two Halves of Life* (San Francisco: Jossey-Bass, 2011).

6. See Alcoholics Anonymous: *Big Book* (New York: AA World Services, 1939), pp. 27–29, 569–570.

7. This is in the twelfth step in *Twelve Steps and Twelve Traditions*. See http://quietmindrecovery.org/AA/step_twelve.htm.

8. "The Spiral of Violence," CD recording by Richard Rohr, available at cacradicalgrace.org.

9. Richard Rohr, *The Naked Now: Learning to See as the Mystics See* (New York: Crossroad, 2009).

CHAPTER TWO

1. Walter Wink, *Engaging the Powers* (Minneapolis: Fortress, 1992), pp. 3–7.

2. Rohr, *The Naked Now*, and Cynthia Bourgeault, *Centering Prayer and Inner Awakening* (Lanham, Md.: Cowley, 2004).

3. Don Richard Riso and Russ Hudson, *The Wisdom of the Enneagram: The Complete Guide to Psychological and Spiritual Growth for the Nine Personality Types* (New York: Bantam, 1999).

4. Ken Wilber, *The Simple Feeling of Being* (Boston: Shambala, 2004); Bill Plotkin, *Nature and the Human Soul* (San Francisco: New World, 2008).

5. Stephen Buhner, *The Fasting Path* (New York: Penguin, 2003).

6. Gerald May, *Addiction and Grace: Love and Spirituality in the Healing of Addictions* (New York: HarperOne, 1988).

CHAPTER THREE

1. See anything by Stephen Levine, along with Kathleen Dowling Singh's *The Grace in Dying* (New York: HarperOne, 1998), and Kerry Walters, *The Art of Dying and Living* (Maryknoll, N.Y.: Orbis, 2011).

2. Rohr, *Falling Upward.*

3. S. Mark Heim, *Saved from Sacrifice: A Theology of the Cross* (Grand Rapids: Eerdmans, 2005).

4. René Girard, *The Girard Reader* (New York: Crossroad, 1996), pp. 69ff.

CHAPTER FOUR

1. "Discharging Your Loyal Soldier," CAC webcast 2010, cacradical-grace.org.

CHAPTER FIVE

1. Joseph Martos, *Doors to the Sacred* (Norwich, U.K.: SCM, 1981), pp. 307ff.

CHAPTER SIX

1. Mihaly Csikszentmihalyi, *Flow: The Psychology of Optimal Experience* (New York: Harper, 1990).

CHAPTER SEVEN

1. Richard Rohr, "True Self/False Self" CD set (Cincinnati: St. Anthony Messenger Press, 2010).

2. Rohr, *Falling Upward,* pp. 25ff.

CHAPTER EIGHT

1. Marshall Rosenberg and Arun Gandhi, *NonViolent Communication* (Encinitas, Calif.: Puddle Dancer, 2003).

CHAPTER NINE

1. See Walter Wink, *The Human Being* (Minneapolis: Augsburg Fortress, 2002).

CHAPTER TEN

1. Rohr, *The Naked Now*, Appendix 3, p. 168.
2. Michael Christensen, ed., *Partakers of the Divine Nature* (Teaneck, N.J.: Farleigh Dickinson University, 2007).

CHAPTER ELEVEN

1. Richard Rohr, *Everything Belongs* (New York: Crossroad, 1999).
2. Rohr, *The Naked Now*, pp. 105 ff.
3. Leo Booth, *When God Becomes a Drug*, 1998 (Cheadle, U.K: SCP, 1998); Robert Neil Minor, *When Religion Is an Addiction* (St. Louis: HumanityWorks!, 2007).
4. See Contemplative Outreach at www.contemplativeoutreach.org and World Community for Christian Meditation www.wccm.org.
5. Thomas Merton, *Journals of Thomas Merton*, August 3, 1958, Vol. III (New York: HarperOne, 1999), p. 121.

CHAPTER TWELVE

1. Bill Plotkin, *Nature and the Human Soul* (Novato, Calif.: New World Library, 2008).
2. Francis McNutt, *The Nearly Perfect Crime* (Grand Rapids: Chosen, 2005).
3. Rohr, *The Naked Now*, chap. 2.
4. Richard Rohr, "The Divine Dance" CD set, available at www.cacradicalgrace.org.

AN UNEXPECTED POSTSCRIPT

1. Origen, "On Prayer," Ante-Nicene Fathers Collection, available at www.ccel.org/ccel/origen/prayer.vii.html?highlight=christ, suffering,human,gospels#highlight.
2. Thomas Hobbes, *The Leviathan*, chap. 13, paragraph 9.
3. Aeschylus, *Agamemnon*, as quoted in Arthur M. Schlesinger, Jr., *Robert Kennedy and His Times* (Boston: Houghton Mifflin, 1978), pp. 875, 1020 n. 84.

Alcoholics Anonymous Big Book. Alcoholics Anonymous World Services, Inc., 1976.

Bien, Thomas and Beverly Bien. *Mindful Recovery: A Spiritual Path to Healing from Addiction.* New York: Wiley, 2002.

Buhner, Stephen Harrod. *The Fasting Path: For Spiritual, Emotional, and Physical Healing and Renewal.* New York: Avery (Penguin), 2003.

Grant, Robert. *The Way of the Wound: A Spirituality of Trauma and Transformation.* Self- published, 1996.

Jay, Frances. *Walking with God through the 12 Steps: What I Learned about Honesty, Healing, Reconciliation and Wholeness.* Chicago: ACTA, 1996.

Johnson, Robert A. *Owning Your Own Shadow: Understanding the Dark Side of the Psyche.* San Francisco: HarperSanFrancisco, 1991.

K, Herb. *Twelve Steps to Spiritual Awakening: Enlightenment for Everyone.* Torrance, Calif.: Capizon, 2010.

Keating, Thomas. *Divine Therapy and Addiction: Centering Prayer and the Twelve Steps.* New York: Lantern, 2009.

———. *Open Mind, Open Heart: The Contemplative Dimension of the Gospel.* New York: Continuum, 1998.

Kegan, Robert, and Lisa Laskow Lahey. *Immunity to Change: How to Overcome It and Unlock the Potential in Yourself and Your Organization (Leadership for the Common Good)*. Boston: Harvard Business School Press, 2009.

Kurtz, Ernest, and Katherine Ketcham. *The Spirituality of Imperfection: Modern Wisdom From Classic Stories*. New York: Bantam, 1992.

May, Gerald. *Addiction and Grace: Love and Spirituality in the Healing of Addictions*. New York: HarperOne, 1998.

Mellon, John C. *Mark as Recovery Story: Alcoholism and the Rhetoric of Gospel Mystery*. Chicago: University of Illinois Press, 1995.

Moltmann, Jürgen. *The Crucified God*. New York: Harper & Row, 1974.

Nakken, Craig. *The Addictive Personality: Understanding the Addictive Process and Compulsive Behavior*. Center City, Minn.: Hazelden, 1996.

Twerski, Abraham J. *Addictive Thinking: Understanding Self-Deception*. Center City, Minn.: Hazelden, 1997.

Webb, Terry. *Tree of Renewed Life: Spiritual Renewal of the Church Through the Twelve-Step Program*. New York: Crossroad, 1992.

Wilber, Ken. *Integral Spirituality: A Startling New Role for Religion in the Modern and Postmodern World*. Boston: Integral (imprint of Shambhala), 2007.

Step outside the pages of *Breathing Under Water* and look within yourself, using this study guide to reinforce each chapter with thoughtful reflection. The study guide will assist you in learning to embrace the energy of each of the Twelve Steps, perhaps even surrender to something greater than yourself. It will become a valuable and indispensable resource as you breathe under water, whether alone or with a small group. Remember that being open to the leading of the Spirit is critical to breathing under water.

CHAPTER ONE:
POWERLESSNESS

1. "People who fail to do it right...are those who often break through to enlightenment and compassion" (pp. 2–3). Think of a time when you felt failure and pain. How did this experience change you?

2. "It is the imperial ego that has to go, and only powerlessness can do the job correctly" (p. 4). What area of your life do you have a need to control?

3. "No one likes to die to who they think they are" (p. 6). Describe yourself. Now think about letting go of that image.

4. "What the ego hates more than anything else in the world is to change" (p. 6). What makes change difficult for you?

CHAPTER TWO:
DESPERATE DESIRING

1. "It takes major surgery...to get head, heart, and body to put down their defenses" (p. 9). In what area of your life do you most strongly resist opening up to new ways of being?

2. "To keep the mind space open, we need some form of contemplative or meditation practice" (p. 11). How can you begin to be still and just *be* in the presence of this Higher Power?

3. "I think your heart needs to be broken, and broken open, at least once to have a heart at all or to have a heart for others" (p. 12). Share a time when your heart was broken. How has this led you to greater compassion?

4. "For many of us the body is more *repressed and denied* than even the mind or the heart" (p. 13). When was the last time you touched someone or that someone touched you? What stops you from doing this?

CHAPTER THREE:
SWEET SURRENDER

1. "Surrender will always feel like dying, and yet it is the necessary path to liberation" (p. 18). What kind of death in your life would bring liberation to you?

2. "What makes so much religion so innocuous,...is that there has seldom been a concrete 'decision to turn our lives over to the care of God'" (p. 20). Have you ever had the experience of turning your life over to God? What happened?

3. "You see, there is a love that sincerely seeks the spiritual good of others, and there is a love that is seeking superiority" (p. 22). From your relationship with others, share an example of both ways of loving.

4. "We have been graced for a truly sweet surrender, if we can *radically accept being radically accepted—for nothing!*" (p. 27). How have you known unconditional love?

CHAPTER FOUR:
A GOOD LAMP

1. "Begin some honest 'shadow boxing' which is at the heart of all spiritual awakening" (pp. 30–31). What part of you do you not want to see?

2. "The goal is...*the struggle itself,* and the encounter and wisdom that comes from it" (p. 31). Share a time when you struggled to face the truth. What happened?

3. "The game is over once we see clearly because evil succeeds only by disguising itself as good, necessary, or helpful" (p. 34). Think of a time when you stopped denying and admitted that some situation or relationship was bad, unnecessary, or harmful. What happened?

4. "God uses our sins in our own favor! God brings us— through failure—from unconsciousness to ever-deeper consciousness and conscience" (p. 35). Think of a time when you admitted failure. How did that experience bring personal change?

Chapter Five:
Accountability IS Sustainability

1. *"You cannot heal what you do not acknowledge"* (p. 39). What personal failure do you find most difficult to acknowledge?

2. "When human beings 'admit' to one another 'the exact nature of their wrongs,' they invariably have a human and humanizing encounter that deeply enriches both sides" (p. 39). What can you admit that will set you, and others, free?

3. "This is the way that God seduces us all into the economy of grace—by loving us in spite of ourselves in the very places where we cannot or will not or dare not love ourselves" (p. 41). Share an experience when someone loved you in spite of what you deserved.

4. "Forgiveness is to let go of our hope for a different or better past" (pp. 48–49). How can you begin to stop replaying hurtful memories?

Chapter Six:
The Chicken or the Egg:
Which Comes First?

1. "We have to fully acknowledge that God alone can do the 'removing'" (p. 52). When have you had an experience of letting go and letting God?

2. "It is a lot of work to get out of the way and allow that grace to fully operate and liberate" (p. 52). When have you gotten in God's way?

3. "We must first fully own and admit that we have 'defects of character,' but then equally, step back and do nothing about it, as it were, *until we are 'entirely ready' to let God do the job*" (p. 54). How has God repaired some of your personal damage without any effort on your part?

4. "It seems we must both surrender and take responsibility" (p. 56). How does this quotation express itself in the ability to dance with a partner? What does this analogy have to say about recovery from addictions?

CHAPTER SEVEN:
WHY DO WE NEED TO ASK?

1. *"We ask not to change God but to change ourselves. We pray to form a living relationship, not to get things done"* (p. 60). How have your prayers changed throughout your life?

2. "Prayer is...*a synergy which creates a result larger than the exchange itself"* (p. 61). How are prayer and grace linked? How would you describe grace?

3. "Jesus told us all to stay in the position of a beggar, a petitioner, a radical dependent, which is always spiritually true, if we are honest" (p. 62). What does it mean to you to be radically dependent?

4. "Life is a gift, totally given to you without cost" (p. 65). What will it take for you to see everything as gift and be grateful with your life?

CHAPTER EIGHT:
PAYBACK TIME

1. "'Amazing Grace' is not a way to avoid honest human relationships, but to redo them—but now gracefully—for the
   liberation of both sides" (p. 69). What relationship would
   you like to redo?

2. *"It is a self-serving concern to alleviate just your own guilt; it is a
   loving question to say, 'How can I free others from theirs?'"* (p.
   71). Remember a time when someone asked your forgiveness to salve their own guilt. How did you feel?

3. "Step 8 is a marvelous tool...for very practical incarnation,
   which keeps Christianity grounded, honest, and focused on
   saving others instead of just ourselves" (p. 72). Remember
   a time when you offered an apology out of real concern
   and love for the other. How did you feel?

4. "Making such a list will change your foundational consciousness from one of feeding resentments to a mind that
   is both grateful and humble" (p. 74). Who is that one
   person you find most difficult to forgive? What can you do
   to want to ask for forgiveness and receive it?

Chapter Nine:
Skillful Means

1. "I am afraid that commonsense wisdom, or skillful means, is no longer common sense. We are a culture with many elderly people but not so many elders passing on wisdom" (p. 76). Who has been an elder, a wise mentor, in your life?

2. "Jesus was a master of teaching skillful means, especially in his Sermon of the Mount, and in many of his parables and one-liners" (p. 76). What saying of Jesus is most important to you?

3. "One often needs time, discernment, and good advice from others before one knows *the when, how, who, and where* to apologize or make amends" (p. 78). Share a time when waiting to apologize paid off.

4. "Skillful means is not just to make amends but to make amends in ways that 'do not injure others'" (p. 80). When did you act too hastily to correct a mistake? What happened?

CHAPTER TEN:
IS THIS OVERKILL?

1. "You must step back from your compulsiveness, and your attachment to yourself, to be truly conscious" (p. 85). What are some ways you can begin to be conscious?

2. "Most people...are rather totally identified with their own thoughts, feelings, and compulsive patterns of perception" (p. 85). How does detachment help you to separate yourself from your feelings, thoughts, and compulsive patterns of perception?

3. "Most churches gave people the impression they would 'get' the Holy Spirit as a reward for good behavior" (p. 88). How does the Holy Spirit act in your life as a Divine Guide and Teacher?

4. "Once we see our inherent dignity clearly, the game of evil and addiction begins to collapse" (p. 90). When is a time that evil won out in your life? What has changed to lead you to good?

CHAPTER ELEVEN:
AN ALTERNATIVE MIND

1. "Most people do not see things as they *are,* they see things as *they* are!" (p. 95). What blinds you from seeing things through the lens of truth?

2. "God cannot directly answer such prayers, because frankly, *they are usually for the wrong thing and from the wrong self*" (p. 96). When did God not answer your prayer? What happened?

3. "Basically prayer is an exercise in *divine participation*—you opting in and God always there!" (p. 97). When have you experienced God's presence in prayer?

4. "People's willingness to find God in their own struggle with life—*and let it change them*—is their deepest and truest obedience to God's eternal will" (p. 103). What does it mean to you when you hear people say, "It's God's will"?

CHAPTER TWELVE:
WHAT COMES AROUND MUST GO AROUND

1. "[Jesus]...knew we had to hand the message over before we really understood it or could appreciate it ourselves" (p. 107). When have you taught someone something and wound up learning more than you taught?

2. "Until we have found our own ground and connection to the Whole, we are all unsettled and grouchy" (p. 113). When have you been "unsettled and grouchy"? What caused these feelings? How could a connection with "the Whole" make a difference at such times?

3. "Addiction is a spiritual disease, a disease of the soul... which is ironically the necessary beginning of any spiritual path" (p. 115). How is addiction a "happy fault"?

4. "I am told that in the Hebrew Bible there is really only one sin, and the one and only sin is *idolatry*: making something a god that is not God" (p. 117). What do you think about more than anything else? Could this be a "god"?

About the Author

Richard Rohr is a globally recognized Catholic and Christian teacher focusing on mystical and transformational traditions and is the founder and director of the Center for Action and Contemplation in Albuquerque, New Mexico, home of the Rohr Institute. He is the author of more than twenty books, including *Yes, And... Daily Meditations; Silent Compassion: Finding God in Contemplation; Immortal Diamond: The Search for Our True Self; Falling Upward: A Spirituality for the Two Halves of Life;* and *Breathing Under Water: Spirituality and the Twelve Steps.*